Kill Em Pamela A Collection of True Crime

Anita Caldwell

Published by Trellis Publishing, 2021.

While every precaution has been taken in the preparation of this book, the publisher assumes no responsibility for errors or omissions, or for damages resulting from the use of the information contained herein.

KILL EM PAMELA A COLLECTION OF TRUE CRIME

First edition. June 29, 2021.

ISBN: 979-8224910311

Written by Anita Caldwell.

KILL 'EM PAMELA
TALES OF WOMEN WHO KILL

ANITA CALDWELL

PAMELA PHILLIPS

Pamela Phillips, known as Pam, is currently serving life in jail for killing her ex-husband. But, is the former wealthy socialite really capable of murder? And why did it take almost 18 years for her to get caught?

Pam's early life was relatively unremarkable. She was born in 1958 to a wealthy family who had a rather frivolous lifestyle. Pam's father was short tempered and drank too much, whereas her mother was a calm and collected woman, who rarely showed any emotion. Perhaps, this combination gave Pam a steely edge and a hunger for the high life. For many years though, Pam seemed like a perfectly normal, ambitious woman. She was very beautiful and achieved a successful career as a real estate agent, growing to be worth between 1 and 2 million dollars.

Pam married young, but after a short time she divorced and became very involved in the Arizona social scene. It was in 1985, that she first laid eyes on Gary Triano. Triano was a successful businessman. He had earned his fortune investing in Native American Bingo halls. Triano was well known and well connected in Arizona. He had many wealthy friends, including Donald Trump. Pam was immediately attracted to Triano and his way of life. The pair began socialising regularly, often at parties held by Triano and his then wife, Mary Cram. Pam and Triano had an ongoing affair, which eventually resulted in Triano making the biggest mistake of his life. While Cram was abroad with the couple's two children, Heather and Brian, Triano messaged her to say that he was filing for divorce.

Less than a year later, Pam and Triano got married. The well off, attractive couple appeared to have it all; close friends described Triano as smitten. They married on a yacht in San Diego. The wedding was an extremely flashy, black-tie event, where guests could sample any drink imaginable.

The following years were dedicated to partying and travelling with other Arizona elites. Pam and Triano purchased a beautiful home in the poshest part of town. They also had two children together, Trevor and Lois. Though Pam has since described Triano as abusive, obsessive and controlling, friends say that at the time she seemed very happy.

In the late 1980s, things started to go wrong. The financial fortunes of Tucson, Arizona, began to change. The real estate market crashed and many of Triano's investments failed. He quickly started developing some serious debts. In the early 1990s, Triano was dealt the biggest blow. The laws around gaming and Bingo halls changed, Native Americans were able to start claiming all the money earnt on the reservations, as their own. Triano was cut out. His earnings plummeted; losing as much as 93% of his income in one year. Triano was a man who borrowed from other individuals, rather than banks. Unable to pay his debts, Triano made quite a few enemies. In particular, a group of Northern Mexican investors that threatened to kill him if he filed for bankruptcy. A desperate Triano also made a dodgy deal with wealthy drug addict, Neil McNeice, another mobster who wanted to have Triano killed. All in all, Triano became a very unpopular guy. Despite various warnings, he filed for bankruptcy in 1994.

Pam was shocked. She had no idea about the true extent of Triano's financial problems. After he claimed bankruptcy however, everything began to come out. Pam learned of Triano's significant debts, totalling around $26 million, including owing his ex-wife $1.8 million and his attorney $97,000. Triano also had 74 pending lawsuits. The man was clearly in dire straits, and Pam was horrified. She had entered the marriage as a successful business woman, worth around 2 million dollars. But, during their time together, Pam had stopped working in order to raise the couple's two children. She later claimed that Triano pressured her to do this. She was about to be ruined. Pam stated that when Triano lost all his money, he became paranoid and extremely hard to live with. Whether or not this is true is extremely hard to say, maybe Pam just didn't want to be involved in Triano's embarrassing downfall. Either way, shortly after discovering the debts, Pam filed for divorce.

The divorce was finalised very quickly – in less than a month. Pam was awarded the house. Supposedly wanting to ditch her newly acquired bad reputation, Pam left Tucson. In an underhand move, she sold the marital house while Triano was away. She pocketed the $300,000 proceeds and in 1994, fled to Aspen with the couple's two children. Triano was left alone and in severe debt in Arizona.

In Aspen, Pam and the children moved to a very affluent area. But, she was struggling to pay the bills and maintain the lifestyle she was used to. Pam wanted to develop a new reputation away from Triano. So, even though she could not afford it, she continued to attend the fancy parties and socialised with the richest members of the Aspen community. Pam tried to get back into real estate, but this proved harder than anticipated because she didn't have the same well established connections as in Arizona. Pam started her own business, Star Babies, predicting the futures of new-borns. She firmly believed that this business could be worth millions, but she needed help.

This is when Pam met Ron Young. Young was supposedly working as a business consultant, although this doesn't appear to have been official. Young helped Pam with her finances, including with the Star Babies business. The two developed a romantic relationship and Young also became involved in Pam's ongoing communications with Triano about the divorce and money. Pam regularly complained about Triano not paying her enough in child support and maintenance. Young tried to help with this and saw Triano as an obstacle. Ron Young was very intelligent, but he was not particularly handsome or wealthy. Many friends wondered about Pam's motivations for the relationship; Young was not her usual type, so perhaps she had something else to gain from him.

By April 1996, Pam was going off Ron Young. Two separate reports had been made to police about Young, accusing him of fraud offences.

Pam herself then contacted the police about him, claiming that he was using her credit card and stealing money from the Star Babies business. Aspen detective, James Crowley, tried to locate Young, but he had disappeared. It transpired that a van was rented in Young's name from Aspen airport, but nobody knew where he had gone. An arrest warrant was issued due to the outstanding forgery charges.

Several months later, detective Crowley received a call from California – the van rented by Young had been located. Young mistakenly left the van near his parent's house and it had been impounded. When he attempted to recover the van, he was informed that the police had been contacted and were on their way. Upon hearing this, Young fled, abandoning the vehicle and its contents. Crowley flew to California to inspect the van and found several intriguing items inside. Such items included: papers from the Star Babies business, documents about Pam and Triano's divorce, a list of people close to Triano, maps of Tucson and hotel receipts in a fake name, also from Tucson. In addition, Crowley found a stolen Arizona licence plate and a sawn off shot gun. These things all seemed highly suspicious to Crowley and suggested that, for whatever reason, Young had been stalking Triano. Despite a wide police search, Young was still untraceable. There was little police could do.

Only two weeks after the discovery of Young's van, headline news stories appeared about a murder in Arizona.

On the 1st November 1996, Gary Triano had played a long round of golf with some friends at La Paloma Country Club. Triano was a member and regularly played 18 holes. Friends state that he was on the verge of being kicked out though, due to not being able to pay the membership fees. After the round of golf, Triano casually walked back to his Lincoln Town car. It was days away from his 53rd birthday and he was planning to celebrate in style. However, someone was waiting for Triano in the car park that day, finger poised. As he climbed into the vehicle, Triano noticed a blue bag that he didn't recognise on the passenger seat next to him. Curious, he reached over to investigate. At that moment, a bomb detonated, blowing the roof off the car and shooting the wind shield over 70 feet. Gary Triano was killed instantly, his wrist watch stopped at 5.38pm.

Emergency vehicles arrived quickly on the scene, but there was nothing they could do to help Triano. The local community of Tucson was in shock. No one could believe that a car bombing would take place there, especially at the most prestigious spot in town. Rumours started spreading that it must be an organised crime job; maybe the Mexican Mafia, or some other criminal that Triano owed money to.

Detective James Gamber collected evidence at the crime scene. Shrapnel and debris were everywhere, the first job was to separate pieces of the bomb from car parts. Eventually the bomb squad claimed that the device was a simple pipe bomb, detonated using a close range remote control from within a quarter of a mile. This meant that the killer was very nearby, probably within the car park, when the explosion was triggered. Although there were many rumours that it was a mob hit, the police had their doubts. The device was clearly built by an amateur, whereas organized crime groups usually employed experts for that type of job. Things didn't quite add up for detective Gamber.

When detective James Crowley in Aspen saw the news stories about Triano's murder, he instantly thought of the mysterious contents of Young's van. Wandering if the two incidents were connected, Crowley called police in Tucson to report his previous findings.

Pam, who was still living in Aspen, was questioned about her relationship with Young. She claimed that there had been no romantic feelings between the two of them, and that he had simply helped her out with financial advice for the Star Babies business. Pam also denied any knowledge of why Young would have suspicious items in his van and confirmed that she did not know his current whereabouts. Detectives could pin Young in Tucson in June and July 1996, thanks to documents found in the van, but they had no real evidence that he had been there in November when the murder was committed. Police did want to question Young in relation to the murder though, particularly because he had no other known connections with Tucson —so why would he get a hotel room there under a fake name? But, still, Young could not be found.

Pam herself was questioned further when detectives discovered that she was the beneficiary of a 2 million dollar life insurance pay out. However, Pam was very cooperative with police and there was nothing to suggest that she was a suspect. With no further leads, and police unable to locate Young, the case went cold.

Pam received the 2 million dollar life insurance money a couple of months after Triano's murder. She bought a large house in the wealthy neighbourhood of Meadowood, Aspen, and spent a significant amount remodelling it. Her lifestyle remained frivolous; partying, travelling, and skiing a lot. She was now able to fund her socialite habits comfortably again. Ten years passed in this manner, with no sign of Young, and Pam living a charmed life thanks to her ex-husbands murder.

In 2005, detective James Gamber, Pima County Sheriff, was assigned to work on unsolved murder cases. He had also worked on the original inquiry into Triano's murder, and felt compelled to look at the case again. There were over 300,000 pages about the car bombing to search through. Having checked everything thoroughly, Gamber concluded that there was only one line of inquiry that hadn't been followed through, one suspect that Gamber couldn't eliminate, and that was Ron Young. By this time, Young had been a fugitive for 9 years. Gamber contacted the popular show *America's Most Wanted* and persuaded them to run a show about Young. The episode aired on the 19th November 2005.

Following the show, police received a number of calls about Young. Most notably, one call was from his chiropractor in Florida, who had recognised him immediately. The chiropractor informed police that

Young actually had an upcoming appointment scheduled. Police moved quickly, and on the date of Young's appointment, they were sat in wait. Florida police were then able to arrest Young on outstanding fraud charges.

Young spent 10 months in jail in Florida for fraud, before police were able to question him about the murder of Gary Triano. Young gave police permission to search his house, storage, and car. This turned out to be quite a bizarre experience for police. It quickly became apparent that Young was obsessed with keeping records, noting down interactions, recording phone conversations, and saving emails. His house was a veritable treasure trove of evidence. Of course, it took police a while to comb through everything. But what they eventually found turned out to be very incriminating; it implicated not only Young, but also Pam Phillips in the murder of Triano.

A large number of cassette tapes held recordings of phone conversations between Young and Pam. There were over 500 calls recorded, spanning a time frame of 8 years. In addition to the voice recordings, there were also 100 saved emails between the two. In almost all their conversations, Pam and Young talked about their favourite topic – money. Police realised that Pam had been regularly sending money to Young. She would send cash via FedEx, and then call Young to inform him of the amount and the tracking number. Incredibly, Young recorded all of these calls – pretty much gathering the required evidence for police. Young even filled in spreadsheets, keeping track of the total amount of money that Pam had sent him. Overall, 44 transactions had been completed. Police found this highly suspicious, particularly because the amount of money discussed by Pam and Young always added up to 2 million, the same amount that Pam received in life insurance for Triano. It sounded like the pair had a pre-existing agreement. There were several points at which Pam and Young argued; during one episode Young even accused Pam of murder and threatened that she would end up in a women's prison. It seemed that Pam had fallen behind with the payments and Young was very angry about it. As far as police could see, there was only one explanation for what was said in the recordings and the transfer of so much money. On the 16th October 2008, Pam and Young were indicted for first degree murder.

Police ran into new problems when they tried to track down Pam. It turned out that she had gone to visit her daughter, who was at college in Switzerland. Upon hearing of Young's arrest and her own indictment, she failed to return. Switzerland would not extradite suspects who were facing cases in which they could be given the death penalty. So, for a time, Pam was safe in Switzerland. She even struck up a new relationship with a wealthy man. They stayed together on the shore of the stunning Lake Lugano. But Pam's fortunes were soon to change.

It was announced that the death penalty was being dropped, meaning that Switzerland could extradite Pam. However, the announcement was made publicly, and Pam was a step ahead of the Swiss police. She was now a fugitive, on the run in Europe.

Meanwhile, Young was put on trial in Tucson, Arizona. The prosecution leaned heavily on the cassette tapes found among Young's possessions. Young pleaded not guilty, saying that he left Aspen in 1996 on a driving holiday with his son. Then, when Young realised he was facing charges of fraud, he didn't think it was a big deal and did not return. Despite having been missing for 9 long years, Young claimed that he wasn't hiding at all, and had instead just been going about an ordinary life in Florida. When questioned about the 2 million dollars discussed in the calls with Pam, he simply explained that it was nothing to do with Triano's life insurance. Young stated that the amount just referred to some equity in real estate that he believed he was owed a portion of. The defence also pointed out that there was no concrete evidence placing Young in Tucson in November 1996. But, despite pleading not guilty, in March 2010, Young was found guilty of first degree murder. The strong circumstantial evidence proved to be enough for the jury to agree. Young appeared to be extremely shocked by this decision. Six weeks later, he was sentenced to two back to back life sentences.

During Young's trial, police felt significant pressure to find Pam. Finally, thanks to European police and the intervention of Interpol, they were able to do so. Pam was discovered in Lichtenstein, before being tracked as she travelled to Vienna, Austria. This is where she was apprehended, on an American arrest warrant.

In July 2010, Pam was returned to Tucson. Her appearance had changed drastically, she looked much older and a little dishevelled. Pam was deemed unfit to stand trial, due to mental health problems. She was held at Pima County Jail, with a 5 million dollar bail set, while she received psychiatric treatment. Eventually, in October 2012, Pam was given the all clear, and a date could be set for the trial.

Pam was charged with first degree murder and conspiracy to commit murder. Her trial began on the 18th February 2014. The trial lasted for a total of 7 weeks, during which the jury heard entirely opposing arguments from the prosecution and the defence.

Again, the prosecution relied almost entirely on the circumstantial evidence provided by Ron Young's records. Pam was painted as someone who lacks empathy and is motivated only by greed. The defence saw it very differently; claiming that the only thing the prosecution had proved was that Pam and Young had some kind of financial link. There were no other facts. Pam's attorney, Paul Eckerstrom, pointed out that Pam wasn't even the one paying for Triano's life insurance – that had fallen to a friend in Aspen during Pam's earlier financial troubles. In addition, the insurance payment directly before Triano's death was missed, forgotten. This is an unlikely mistake to make if you were planning a murder, surely the suspect would have done everything possible to ensure that the insurance would actually be paid.

The defence also refer to the findings from DNA tests done on the pipe bomb, saying that the tests excluded Young from being the builder and perpetrator. This would naturally call into question Pam's involvement too.

The defence took their argument even further by providing an alternative suspect, Neil McNeice. A wealthy man who was addicted to cocaine and heroin, McNeice had already passed away in 2002. He was never fully investigated, and the defence claimed that this was an error on the part of the police. The story went that Triano had needed some cash, so he struck a deal with Neil McNeice, selling him a $250,000 diamond engagement ring. The problem was that the ring was a fake and only really worth around $9000. When McNeice realised this, he apparently flew into a rage, raving about how he would have Triano killed. McNeice's doctor, Lawrence D'Antonio, corroborated this, explaining that he had heard McNeice threaten to kill Triano on several separate occasions. D'Antonio clearly believed that McNeice was behind the murder.

Finally, the defence argued that Young's tapes had never been authenticated and that if the jury listened to them carefully all the way through, a different picture would be formed. Eckerstrom said that when Young accused Pam of murder, he was not talking about Triano, but about himself. Young was suffering from an illness at the time and needed the money for healthcare. Also, according to Eckerstrom, the 2 million dollars discussed was from real estate investments, as Young claimed in his trial. Eckerstrom gave an impassioned defence of Pam, and advocated for Young's innocence too, but the prosecution were about to react strongly.

With regards to the McNeice argument, prosecutors pointed out that the initial betrayal with the ring had taken place in 1991. It was a long time to wait to commit murder, especially for a powerful man who could have ordered something like that to happen very quickly. Prosecutors said that the defence had only shown that McNeice was angry with Triano, they had given no evidence that he was actually involved in the murder.

Next, the prosecution called their most prominent witness, an old friend of Pam's, Laura Chapman. Chapman's account would prove to be a deciding factor in the outcome of the trial. Chapman claimed that when Pam was living in Aspen, Triano went to her house one night and threatened her. The ex-husband and wife ended up having a huge argument. After Triano left, Pam apparently called Chapman and another friend, who both went to see if she was OK. Whilst they tried to console Pam, she told them about the 2 million dollar life insurance policy and said that she should just hire a hitman and have Triano killed. When Chapman learned what happened on the 1st November 1996, her first thought was one of horror that Pam had followed through with her plan. Chapman had apparently spent the following years living in fear that if she spoke about Pam's threat, something would happen to her.

Defence lawyers tried to claim that Pam had only said those things because she was upset and scared after the fiery argument with Triano. Also, the other friend who attended Pam's house that night has no apparent recollection of Pam talking about the life insurance and threatening to kill Triano. The prosecution and Chapman argued that the other friend is simply too afraid to testify against Pam.

In the closing statements, prosecutor Rick Unklesbay stated that Young was "not getting paid for business advice that she never takes, he's getting paid for murder."

After a long trial, the jury only took 3 days to decide Pam's fate. On the 8th April 2014, she was found guilty of murder. Sentencing took place on the 22nd May 2014. Pam entered the courtroom in shackles and an orange jumpsuit, not quite the designer brands that she was accustomed to. The prosecution pushed for the maximum sentence. Pam was awarded natural life in prison, with no possibility of parole.

Judge Richard Fields stressed that he had "no residual doubt" about Pam's guilt.

Upon hearing her sentence, Pam stood and addressed the court. She repeatedly claimed to be innocent and described the whole experience as a nightmare. Defence lawyer, Eckerstrom, also remains convinced of Pam's innocence, "this is one of the hardest things I have ever had to do in my career, watch my client be sentenced when I know she is innocent." Eckerstrom described Pam's conviction as an injustice.

On the contrary, Heather Triano, Gary Triano's daughter from his first marriage, believes that justice has been served. She said that "Pam, who at one time was my stepmother and my friend, destroyed lives due to her greed and love of money." Trevor and Lois Triano, Pam's children, were not in the courtroom. When asked about them, Heather stated that "Pam's lack of thought for her own children is appalling." Heather Triano and other family members maintain that Gary Triano was a family man who loved his children. This is very different from Pam's account of an abusive, paranoid man, heavily involved in the Arizona mob scene.

Eckerstrom continues to fight and appeal Pam's case. But, nearly 18 years after the murder of Gary Triano, Pam Phillips was incarcerated and it is unlikely that she will ever be released.

WENDI ANDRIANO THE KILLER

GERI AGAJANIAN

Chapter 1

A dying husband needs a devoted wife. But when love runs out, marriage becomes a burden.

On October 8, 2000, Wendi Andriano snapped. She had played the part of devoted wife to her terminally ill husband, Joe Andriano, for years, but when the love left their marriage, so did Wendi's patience for her husband's eventual demise.

Wendi had a plan to help nudge nature along, and when her plan b expired, she took matters directly into her own hands and bludgeoned him to death.

Wendi first tried to poison her husband by spiking his last meal, a homemade beef stew, with sodium azide, but Joe Andriano did not ingest enough to kill him, only enough to vomit it back up. Wendi then grabbed the nearest object, a bar stool, and beat her dying husband over the head so many times that parts of his brain became exposed.

After thinking she had successfully killed her husband twice, Wendi then realized that Joe was still breathing, so she took a knife from the family kitchen and stabbed him in the side of the throat.

Minutes later, Joe was finally dead.

This bizarre and frantic way Wendi killed her husband isn't the strangest thing about the case though. Known even to Wendi, Joe was due to die from terminal cancer within the next few years anyways.

Why Wendi couldn't wait to kill her husband is an intriguing tale wrought with sex, lies, and strangely, a lack of patience.

Chapter 2

Wendi and Joe Andriano grew up together in the small farming community of Casa Grande, Arizona. But while they both had gone to the same school, they never dated. As a minister's daughter, Wendi's social life was restricted to her father's church. Her celebration for graduating high school was even in the form of a missionary trip to Mexico in 1989. When she returned she took a job at the local clerical hospital.

Wendi met Joe in 1992 through friends. Although when the couple started dating Joe's family found the minister's daughter to be an unusual fit for the loud, outgoing former football player, they all thought she was friendly enough and approved of the match.

Joe worked for a local boat builder. He was very mechanically inclined and was a very good welder. He owned his own boat and took Wendi for several cruises around the local hot spots for speedboats. They were inseparable.

The couple married in January of 1994. Their wedding took place in a baptist church across the street from their shared elementary school. Their reception was at the Elk's club and was populated by their many friends and family. Even after two years of dating, though, Joe's family felt like they didn't know his new bride very well, but Joe seemed to be very happy, so they were happy for him.

Soon after marrying, the couple became business partners when they started a small company that did windshield repair and replacement. The business combined Wendi's office experience with Joe's mechanical experience, skills they both exceeded at, and the business thrived.

The couple hadn't been married a whole year yet before they faced their first major challenge together. That fall, Joe noticed an odd bump on his neck. When he had it tested, he was told it was a non-cancerous benign tumor, but it wasn't long before they were second-guessing the diagnoses. A year after it was removed, the tumor grew back.

A second surgery and round of tests seemed to reconfirm that the tumor was benign, but shortly after Wendi gave birth to a son in 1997, the tumor was back yet again.

The third time the tumor returned, Joe's wife and family were convinced that the tumor had to be cancer. This fear was confirmed in 1998 when Joe underwent surgery to have the bump removed for the fourth time. Joe's pre-surgery chest x-ray showed that not only was the tumor cancerous, but that the cancer had now spread across Joe's throat, chest, and lungs.

The prognosis wasn't good—Joe had a rare form of cancer and while radiation and chemotherapy were standard, there was no guarantee they would work. On top of this, Wendi was also pregnant again and was only months away from giving birth to the couple's second child.

Chapter 3

In an effort to increase Joe's chances of survival while decreasing his suffering, Wendi and Joe decided to pursue holistic treatments before resorting to chemotherapy and radiation. They had been told that chemotherapy and radiation treatments would likely not cure Joe, but they would lengthen his life by a few years; however, these years would be anything from pleasant. The horrific side-effects chemotherapy and radiation treatments cause are well known.

So the Andriano's decided first to try anything from special diets to alternative medical treatments to prayer—anything that had a chance to help Joe. Joe even attended a holistic treatment centre for cancer patients in Colorado for a few weeks where he was surrounded by other men and women facing the same prognosis as him. After seeing the bravery of others in the same position as him, Joe began thinking about his future again and began to see it as bright for the first time in a while.

After Joe returned from his holistic healing getaway with a bright new attitude, the Andriano's decided the next best step would be for Joe to begin chemotherapy treatments. He had begun to crave his future and was ready to take steps to achieve it. Unfortunately, taking these steps meant that Joe needed to quit his welding job as well as his own position in the couple's business.

To help make ends meet, Wendi returned to working for the first time since the birth of the couple's children. She ended up taking multiple jobs and worked long hours while continuing to care for her husband at home. Eventually, Wendi landed a job managing the San

Riva apartment complex in the Ahwatukee foothills, an upscale neighbourhood outside of Phoenix.

Wendi's new job came with some major perks—the salary was above average, which was nice as Wendi was now the family's breadwinner, and it required Wendi to live on site, which meant that the family now lived in a luxury apartment but paid no rent. Wendi's new job also gave her a new life. A large part of her duties as complex manager was arranging social activities for the other residents of the San Riva apartments, who were mostly young, wealthy, single businesspeople.

Every Saturday the complex hosted picnics, pool parties, or late-night socials. The residents even had their own baseball team. Wendi was required to attend every event, which meant Joe was needed to stay home with their two children. Wendi enjoyed this alone time so much that many of the residents at the San Riva had no clue she had a dying husband and two children at home. She partied like she was single.

The first few months at the San Riva went well. Wendi organized mixers and pool parties for the tenants while Joe took care of the kids. Despite being very weak from treatments, he did everything he could, he wanted to do it. He prefered to have his kids around him even when he didn't feel good.

Although they had never gotten close to their daughter-in-law, Joe's parents also pitched in with babysitting so the couple could have time alone together. They didn't get to see each other much as Wendi began spending more and more time at work. Her new job had also given her a new confidence, and she spent many nights out on the town dancing and drinking away her weekday stress with friends. Joe began to fear that Wendi would soon leave him for her new lifestyle, but this fear got sidetracked when his health continued to fail.

In the summer of 2000, when tests revealed his cancer had spread yet again, Joe and Wendi decided to increase the frequency of Joe's chemotherapy. Joe agreed to undergo more treatments, but they quickly took their toll. He lost 15 pounds in the first week alone, and Joe's doctor became concerned. It went from bad to worse very quickly.

By the beginning of October 2000, it became harder and harder to remain optimistic about Joe's chances of beating his cancer. It became apparent it was terminal, but doctors insisted that with treatment Joe could live for several more years.

No one had any idea that Joe would be dead after only the first week of the month. No one, that is, except for one person—Wendi Andriano.

Chapter 4

Just after 2:00 a.m. on October 8, Wendi Andriano called a friend who also lived in the San Riva apartment complex. She told her friend that she needed someone to stay with the kids while she took Joe to the hospital. When the friend arrived, she found Joe on the floor, barely alive.

Joe was on the floor in the fetal position. There was vomit on the floor around him and he couldn't stand up. Wendi confided in her friend that she told Joe that she had called 9-1-1 and paramedics were on the way, but this wasn't true. After seeing Joe in such poor condition, the neighbour urged Wendi to call paramedics. She then went outside to wait for them to arrive while Wendi waiting with her husband.

Wendi did call 9-1-1, but when the EMT's arrived minutes later, she refused to let them or her friend inside the apartment. She said that her husband was dying from terminal cancer and had a do not resuscitate order. Joe was not to receive any medical attention.

Just over an hour later, at 3:30 a.m., Wendi dialed 9-1-1 a second time. The same team of paramedics came to the house. It didn't take them long to realize something wasn't quite right, so they contacted the police department. Both the paramedics and the police were shocked to find out that Joe, who had been terminally ill from cancer for quite some time had died, but not from the cancer that had been slowly killing his body. He died from being repeatedly beaten with a bar stool and from being stabbed in the neck.

When the police opened the front door of the apartment, they were confronted with obvious signs of a deadly struggle. The apartment was in a complete state of disarray, and there was blood everywhere. Blood had been traced throughout the kitchen, the dining room, and the living room of the luxury apartment, and blood had spattered across the walls the ceilings. Lying in the middle of the bloody scene was Joe, with a knife wound in his neck and holes spattered across his visible skull.

While crime scene technicians surveyed the apartment, phoenix police took Wendi down to the station for a formal statement. She was wearing clothes drenched in Joe's blood and was armed with a story that explained how Joe's death had been a complete accident.

In the interrogation room, Wendi told police she and joe had spent the evening in Casa Grande visiting with Joe's parents. They put the kids to bed after they returned home, which was when Joe noticed something odd about Wendi's appearance—she wasn't wearing her wedding ring.

According to Wendi, Joe worked himself into a rage and began accusing her of having an affair. This argument turned into a shoving match, and when Joe grabbed a belt, Wendi grabbed a bar stool and swung. Joe went down on all fours so she hit him again. It was then that she called her neighbour for help. Joe may have been in a terrible state when the neighbour saw him, but according to Wendi when she went outside Joe had gotten back to his feet easily.

Wendi said she denied the EMTs access to the apartment because she and Joe were both embarrassed about the fight, but just minutes after the EMTs left, the fight got physical again.

Wendi said that her husband tried to strangle her with a telephone cord and she defended herself with the first weapon she could get in her hands—a kitchen knife. She was vague about how the knife ended up in Joe's neck though, saying she was holding the knife up when Joe suddenly fell flat on his face. The next thing she knew, blood was spurting everywhere. He must have fallen on the blade, it was simply an accident.

Many things about this story didn't make sense to the police. First of all, the timeline presented in Wendi's story didn't match the accounts of Wendi's neighbour or the EMTs. Wendi's neighbour had seen no evidence of a physical fight when they first entered the apartment—there were no broken bar stools or blood like later when the police arrived. As well, Wendi had few injuries on her body, definitely no injuries that would necessitate self defence in the form of murder.

Joe's illness also shed doubt on Wendi's story. Joe's parents told police that when the Andriano's visited earlier that evening, Joe had been so weak from his treatments that he could barely stand. They had spent the evening doting on their sick son, bringing him any comforts he wanted. If he was too weak to stand, he certainly couldn't have been strong enough to violently attack Wendi.

Police also uncovered a damning piece of evidence from Wendi herself, in a moment when she thought she was all alone. The investigators that had been questioning Wendi left her on her own in the interrogation room for some time while they fact checked some of her statements and checked in with the investigators who were scanning the crime scene for evidence. During this time, Wendi made a phone call to a coworker at the apartment complex and asked them to hide some of her files from the police. This immediately led to a search of Wendi's office where police found evidence that Wendi had in fact killed her husband. She had even been planning it for months.

Chapter 5

While both investigators strongly believed that Wendi Andriano was responsible for Joe's death, they were stumped by her motive. Why would Wendi kill her dying husband? The police didn't know, but they did have one intriguing lead—the phone call Wendi had made from the interrogation room. They were determined to find out what she was trying to hide.

When they searched her office, police discovered that Wendi had been disciplined at work for using her computer to search inappropriate items on the internet while on the clock.She had been conducting research on poisons, and how to use certain poisons to kill people. They also discovered the papers that she had tried to hide—shipping notices for a substance known as sodium azide.

Sodium azide is a lethal substance with a variety of industrial uses including propelling airbags. It is not, however, something that the average person can simply go out and buy. It's not restricted to the point where only certain companies can possess it, but it needs to be bought for a reason—something that an apartment complex didn't have. But based on the information on the shipping invoice, Wendi had found a way around that.

Wendi had created a fictitious business license using the tax ID form for the apartment complex. Using a Xerox machine and an exacto knife, Wendi had removed all information specific to the apartment complex and inserted fictitious information for a fake company.

The business name on the shipping notice was bogus, but the address wasn't. Wendi had the substance delivered to an address in Scottsdale, Arizona in an attempt to distance herself, but that plan didn't work. When the police tracked down the real address on the invoice, workers at the company positively identified Wendi as the person who had come by a couple weeks earlier to pick up a package she had mistakenly had shipped there instead of her own office.

Wendi's coworkers had seen her with a package but that she had been very mysterious with the contents. She refused to tell anyone what was inside. Had this been the sodium azide? And if so, where was it now?

Chapter 6

Suspecting that Wendi had tried to poison Joe with the sodium azide, police took samples of every medication and food they could find in the Andriano's apartment. If Joe had ingested poison, it would have explained the awful state Wendi's friend had seen him in just over an hour before he died. Luckily, the remainders of Joe's last supper, homemade beef stew, still sat in a pot on the stove.

However, police didn't find any evidence of Wendi's mysterious package, or any evidence of the sodium azide itself in Wendi and Joe's apartment. They had just begun to lose hope in finding the poison when they found out Wendi had a storage space in the building that she failed to tell the police about. Hidden behind a stack of boxes in Wendi's storage unit was a small bottle of white powder and a measuring spoon. The white powder was soon identified as sodium azide.

But the storage unit wasn't the only place investigators found the lethal substance—it was also in Joe's stomach contents and in the beef stew on the stove.

While discovering the poison helped police understand that Wendi had been trying to kill her husband, it didn't explain why she had bludgeoned him to death on October 8, 2000. Wendi had spent a lot of time researching poisons and she spent a lot of time manufacturing documents so that she could purchase the poison. It certainly wasn't a spur of the moment decision.

But why would Wendi beat and stab her husband if she had already poisoned him? Prosecutors had a theory, one that would cut to the heart of the crime. It was patience—or more precisely, Wendi's lack of it—that had killed Joe in the end.

Wendi had grown tired of waiting for the cancer to kill Joe, so she decided to give nature a little nudge by poisoning his supper. But according to the theory, when Wendi gave Joe the poison, things didn't go quite to plan. Joe hadn't ingested enough poison to kill him when he began vomiting it back up. With her plan quickly failing, Wendi panicked. She snapped.

Now improvising, Wendi beat Joe with the nearest object she could get her hands on—a bar stool. Pathologists were able to conclude that Wendi beat Joe over the head with the stool no less than twenty-four times. This beating did render Joe unconscious, but still didn't kill him so Wendi grabbed a kitchen knife and stabbed him in the part of his body that caused all this trouble in the first place—the side of his neck.

Chapter 7

Ten days after she murdered her husband, Wendi Andriano was formally charged with first degree murder. Wendi's crime was viewed as being especially cruel due to the large amount of suffering Joe had had to endure over several hours thanks to Wendi's actions. Because of this, the prosecutor's on Wendi's trial did the almost unthinkable, they sought the death penalty.

When Wendi a walked into the Arizona courtroom on September 9, 2004 she looked vastly different from the perky apartment manager that the residents of the San Riva apartments used to know.

At the time of the killing she had been blonde, she had short hair, and generally appeared to be much younger and cute than the individual who appeared in court with long dark hair and thick glasses. Previously, she had liked to look good and show her figure so her conservative dress at the trial was certainly different from the look her friends were used to seeing. She was trying to look more conservative, more innocent.

She had had plenty of time to perfect her new look—it had taken prosecutors almost four years to bring the case to trial. It had been postponed about 12 times before it was finally brought before a judge and jury.

In their opening statement, prosecutors reminded the jury that at the time of the murder Wendi had been anything but the perfect mother or wife she claimed to have been. She had been someone who had no disregard for her husband at all. While her husband was dying, she had gone out partying and started affairs, and when his condition worsened, and it began to cramp her style, she turned to poison.

Wendi didn't like her new role as family breadwinner, especially with the loss of Joe's income, and with rising medical bills, the family was in the worst financial state they had ever been in. Wendi had thought she was going to be able to be a stay-at-home-mom for the rest of her life, and she did not adjust well to her return to the workforce. So Wendi had found an out.

Although Joe did not have any life insurance, even though Wendi had asked several friends to pretend to be Joe in medical exams so he could be insured, Joe had filed a malpractice suit against his former doctor who had continually told him his tumor was benign when it was in fact spreading throughout his body. If Joe died and the lawsuit went through, Wendi would likely walk away with a multi-million dollar settlement.

More than money though, Wendi had wanted freedom. She wanted the freedom to be single again, she wanted freedom to the ball-and-chain who was slowly dragging her spirit into his grave along with himself. Wendi wanted to not have to care about her dying husband anymore, who was too weak to provide her with any love.

Wendi maintained her plea of innocence throughout the trial, and her defence team attempted to prove she had been the victim of abuse not only on the night of Joe's death but also throughout the couple's entire marriage. To explain the poison, Wendi told the court that Joe had been the one who had grown tired of waiting for the cancer to end his life, and had asked Wendi to help him do it himself.

On the witness stand Wendi said that Joe had willingly taken the poison, but she also stuck by the story that she had originally told police, that Joe had suspected an affair and became enraged when she affirmed them. He became deranged and attacked her, starting the bloody fight. Wendi claimed Joe had died during the ensuing struggle.

Wendi's story wasn't enough to convince the court though, and on November 18, 2004 she was found guilty of the crime. It had taken the jury only two-and-a-half-hours to come to its unanimous decision. Six years after her husband joe had been diagnosed with terminal cancer, Wendi Andriano faced a possible death sentence of her own.

On December 20, 2004, the jurors assigned to Wendi Andriano's case met and decided on Wendi's fate—it would be death for Ms Andriano. Wendi, along with most of the courtroom, was aghast. Even Joe's family was shocked by the decision. Wendi Andriano became the second ever woman to be put on death row in Arizona, a state that reserves the death penalty for the worst of the worst.

Wendi Andriano has since attempted to appeal the court's decision, but as of early 2017, all attempts have been denied and Wendi continues to wait on death row. Wendi and Joe's children now live with Joe's parents, who continue to mourn the loss of their beloved son.

Joe Andriano's death was especially long, and especially cruel, but no happy ending was found when Wendi was sentenced to her own death. Many view the conclusion of this case to be the saddest possible outcome. On October 8, 2000, two lives were lost, and two children were left without parents.

WHEN A PATIENT KILLS HER THERAPIST

27

ANA BENSON

Relationships with staggering age gaps are not very uncommon, but it is certainly odd when therapists and patients become enamored with each other. It is a unique connection because one side is revealing a lot about themselves in hopes of resolving their most intimate problems. But Dr. Felix Polk wasn't a standard therapist and he thought that opening up about his private life would make his patients regard him as a friend.

Susan and Felix Polk did raise a lot of eyebrows when they announced their engagement, and it was not solely because of the age difference. The two of them started their love affair when she was just a troubled teenager and he was married to another woman. Unfortunately, their story didn't have a happy ending. Susan was a mental patient after all, and it seemed like Felix simply couldn't help her, no matter what he tried. So what drove this woman to murder her husband? How did their relationship really start and was it ever healthy? Or did Dr. Felix Polk use his authority to control Susan from a very early age, resulting in her breakdown?

Early life

Susan Polk was born on January 25th, 1957 and she lived with her family in Oakland, California. Her upbringing was typical up until the point when Susan's parents told her they were getting divorced. Susan was already in her teens and didn't accept the news well. The whole situation was a bit of a shock to her because she was sure that the separation will change her entire life. She started acting out in school, causing various types of trouble. This led her mother to worry about Susan because she blamed the divorce for the daughter's bad behavior. Not to forget that Susan stopped spending time with her parents and she experienced severe mood swings.

Susan started seeing the school therapist after a panic attack she had while in class. She was attending Clayton Valley High School in Concord, California at the time. Everyone around her was worried and thought that she could benefit from talking to someone about her issues. The school therapist encouraged Susan to open up and she started making odd allegations about her parents. It seemed like the problems were more intense than the therapist could handle, so they recommended a specialist who focused on adolescent behavior only – Dr. Frank "Felix" Polk.

Dr. Frank "Felix" Polk worked at Berkley and he was known for his revolutionary methods of treating his patients. The conversations were never one-sided, and Felix didn't shy away from sharing details of his own personal life during the therapy sessions. After all, he started studying psychology at the time when the experts working in that field wanted to try out other ways of dealing with mental illnesses. Even though Felix's approach was not a standard doctor-patient relationship, it appeared that it was working since nobody ever complained.

Susan attended the first therapy session with Dr. Polk sometime in 1972 when she was fifteen years old. She liked her therapist, and the two seemingly understood each other well. Dr. Felix Polk was significantly older than Susan but they managed to find the common grounds. He was married at the time and already had two children with his wife. However, Susan will later reveal that they apparently did have sexual relations when she started her therapy sessions and that Dr. Polk was immediately interested in her. But their relationship would have been illegal since Susan was still a minor.

Susan was doing better and she focused on her school work. Her grades did improve and she wasn't as preoccupied with her parents' divorce as before. She got accepted to Mills College which is located in the Oakland Hills where she spent a couple of years. Susan then moved on to San Francisco State University in the pursuit of an academic degree. She graduated but continued to correspond with her old therapist. Felix Polk wasn't her doctor anymore, but Susan was still going through a lot and her old mental problems returned. She was still having panic attacks while attending the university and Dr. Polk was always there for her. He was teaching at California Graduate School of Family Psychology.

Felix Polk was married to a well-known pianist Sharon Mann and the two got divorced in 1982. It was clear that he was attracted to Susan, and wanted to be in a relationship with her instead. They made it official the same year. Their families were a bit shocked because Felix Polk was a lot older than Susan and they were an unlikely couple. As a matter of fact, Felix was fifty while Susan was only twenty-five on the day of their wedding. But this didn't stop them at all. The couple was very affectionate and they adored each other. They moved to Orinda, California which was a popular location for wealthy families. Susan and Felix were prominent figures in the community and everyone knew them. After all, Felix was already an established psychotherapist who was worth millions of dollars. They had a stable family life and Susan gave birth to three boys during the period they were together.

While everything did look idyllic from the outside, Susan was still having a lot of problems, and Felix did try to help her. It will be discovered later on that Susan was the abusive one in the marriage, even though she did her best to paint Felix as an aggressor. Felix Polk was experienced in dealing with similar patients and he tried to help his wife as best as he could, but Susan was beyond repair. So after almost twenty years of marriage, Susan filed for a divorce from Felix Polk in 2001. Her reasoning was that she was being abused by her husband. Susan quickly packed up her belongings and moved out of their house, leaving her children with their father. Her plan was to move to Montana. The couple appeared in front of a judge to finalize the separation and Felix received the custody of Eli, Gabriel, and Adam. He also got the house and the property the couple shared.

Susan was not used to living on her own, and she quickly ran out of the money. Her plan to move out of the state failed and she had nowhere to go. So Susan simply walked back into their family home and pretended like nothing happened. Felix was confused, but he didn't throw his ex-wife out of the house. He knew that she had mental problems and accepted the fact that she is now living with him and their youngest son. Susan wanted the house to herself, so she moved Felix into the pool house. Once again, Felix did not say a word to Susan, but he did confess to their friends that he was scared of his wife. Her behavior was getting stranger and he was actually afraid for his life. Nobody could have predicted that the situation would escalate just a couple of weeks after Susan's return.

The discovery of the body

On the morning of October 14th, 2002, Susan picked up her son Gabriel from his high school. The boy was in trouble because he missed weeks and weeks of school in the previous months. Susan was not a strict parent, and it seemed like she didn't mind that her son wasn't going to classes regularly. The two of them decided to grab a bite to eat at a nearby restaurant before they returned to their home in Orinda. Gabriel had plans with his father later that afternoon. Felix promised to take the boy to a baseball game and Gabriel was quite excited about it. It was an important event he didn't want to miss.

Once they came back home, Susan quickly left Gabriel alone to wait for his father. He hung around the house, not doing much. Felix failed to pick Gabriel up at 03:00 PM so he called his father's office. No one answered. The boy was getting worried but he didn't want to raise any alarms at the time. His mother returned home in the late afternoon and proceeded to make a family dinner. When Gabriel expressed his concerns about the whereabouts of his father and the fact that he missed their appointment, Susan answered vaguely and she was completely uninterested. She even suggested that Gabriel calls the authorities if he was so worried. She apparently assumed that Felix had a car accident on his way to Orinda and continued to cook.

They ate dinner and watched the baseball game on the TV. The boy noticed that his mother was quiet and didn't speak much. Even though his father's car wasn't in the driveway, Gabriel went to check the pool house just to make sure he is not there. The pool house had some electrical problems so he couldn't turn on the lights as he entered the main room. But it did seem like his father was not inside so he came back into the main house.

His mother was still in the kitchen and he asked her where his dad was. Susan then gave him a very creepy answer: "He is gone." In that moment Gabriel knew that something was very wrong and that his mother might have hurt his father. He was feeling anxious and started going through the house in hopes of finding Felix. He then remembered that they had a flashlight in the kitchen, so he picked it up and went back to the pool house. He turned it on as soon as he opened the door and saw his father laying on his back with a pool of blood around him. The boy was terrified so he screamed and ran back into his room, locking the door behind him. Gabriel was now certain that his mother did this and feared for his own life. He grabbed the phone and called the police, refusing to come outside to meet them.

A couple of minutes after the phone call, Officer Hansen arrived at the Polk residence and Susan greeted him calmly. He informed her that he was there in order to check on Dr. Felix Polk. Susan invited him in and Officer Hansen briefly talked to her. She answered a couple of questions, informing him that she saw her husband a few hours ago and that he was very much alive. Officer Hansen wasn't sure what to think at that point, but he placed handcuffs on her wrists, telling her that it was for everyone's protection. Susan didn't protest – she remained seated in her chair. The responding officer walked to the pool house because Gabriel told the 911 operator that his father's body was in there. Hansen knew that Felix was dead for more than just a couple of hours. His body was starting to change colors, and it was obvious that he was laying on his back for quite a while. Hansen didn't want to disturb the scene of the crime, so he slowly exited the room and called the dispatch telling them that there was indeed a murder victim in the Polk residence.

Officer Hansen informed Susan that her husband was killed and she was not surprised at all. When the detectives and the forensic team arrived, they closed off the pool house and went to examine the body of Dr. Polk. He had multiple stab wounds all over his body, most of them on his chest and around his heart. His death was violent and clearly caused by a sharp object, probably a knife. Susan was the obvious suspect because the murder itself appeared to be fueled by passion. She was taken out of the house, straight into the interrogation room because the detectives were positive that she was the prime suspect.

The arrest and interrogation

Susan was questioned by the detectives working on the case as soon as she arrived at the police station. She appeared composed, but everyone in the room noticed that she was a bit off. While it is typical for a suspect to deny any accusations right away, she caught them off guard with her story. Susan believed that her husband was killed by a hitman because he was working with the Israeli government as a spy. That tale was exaggerated, and nobody believed a single word of her account. They continued to keep her in custody, hoping that she would crack. And she did.

The next day Susan told a different story. Apparently, she did kill her husband in self-defense after he attacked her with a knife. She fought him off, took the blade from his hands, and stabbed him in order to protect herself. Susan mentioned the fact that she was in an abusive marriage and that Felix was often violent towards her. This was enough for the investigators and they were ready to present the case to a judge. Susan was about to go on a trial. In the meantime, she was released on bail and allowed to wait for her trial as a free woman. However, this didn't last for long and she was back in the jail after violating the terms of her release.

Gabriel was also at the police station at the same time, giving the police officers his version of the story. After all, he was the only one present at the house when the murder took place. His older brother

Adam was at the university, but he did call in to talk to Gabriel as soon as he found out what happened. The police also contacted Eli who was at a juvenile facility. While Adam and Gabriel were sure that their mother was guilty of murdering their father Felix, Eli had doubts. He claimed that he was very close to his mother and that she wasn't capable of hurting anyone, especially not Felix. Eli told the police that their parents did have some differences, but they were still devoted to each other. This created a lot of tensions between the brothers themselves, and they ended up choosing sides in the end.

The forensic examination was underway and the evidence did not speak in Susan's favor. The prosecution was preparing to reveal them in front of a judge since Susan didn't provide them with plenty of details. Her confession and the self-defense claim were quite shaky. The case against Susan Polk was solid but no one expected such an intriguing trial. So many unknown things resurfaced in that courtroom, and the entire country was watching attentively.

The trial of Susan Polk

The first trial began on October 17th, 2005. Daniel Horowitz was leading Susan's defense but the entire process was stopped quickly. Horowitz's wife was murdered at the time, and the judge removed him from the case. Susan was thrilled to have Horowitz in her corner at first and wasn't happy with the fact that she would need to find a replacement. She changed her mind quickly and was happy to have him removed from her team. The judge set a new date – February 27th, 2006 and gave Susan enough time to hire a defense lawyer. But Susan decided to let go her remaining team. She refused every suggested lawyer and demanded to be allowed to defend herself. The judge subsequently approved her request.

The jury was selected in February and the trial began in March of 2006. The murder of Dr. Felix Polk attracted a lot of media attention - the entire process was covered by numerous TV crews who waited in front of the courtroom. Both the victim and the accused were intriguing to everyone, and the fact that this crime happened in an affluent neighborhood added an extra layer of interest. Paul Sequeira was the leading prosecutor and he was going head to head with Susan Polk. Keep in mind that Susan appeared as a small and demure woman, but she didn't hesitate to talk back to Sequeira right there in the courtroom.

Her story was slowly expanding as she added more information. Since her initial claim was that her husband was an Israeli spy, she also included the US government conspiracy to get her locked up for a crime she didn't commit. Susan was certain that the crime scene was altered by the investigators just to put the entire blame on her, even though a hired hitman was behind the murder. It appeared that she forgot about her self-defense claim, but she returned to that as well. The media was enjoying the spectacle, and everyone could follow the trial day to day either on the cable television or online.

Susan needed to present herself as a victim so she revealed that Felix Polk seduced her when she was only fifteen years old. Having in mind his unorthodox methods of dealing with his patients, the two of them got to know each other pretty quickly and developed strong feelings. Susan told the courtroom that Felix would often hypnotize her and she felt like it was a form of abuse as well. Apparently, he was able to control her actions and keep her by his side. Susan claimed that when she refused to have an intercourse with Felix as a minor, he drugged and raped her. She felt like she was obliged to continue their relationship after that event. The accusations were never-ending, and she mentioned that he continued to drug and scare their three boys as well. Susan did her best to tarnish her husband's reputation as a well-known and successful psychotherapist.

The trial became even more interesting when the prosecution introduced their witnesses – Gabriel and Adam Polk. They were openly accusing their mother of the murder, describing her as a violent and controlling person who abused the whole family. Adam was visibly shaken and he said the following while testifying on the stand: "We all lose here. Felix is no longer in our lives and we miss him terribly." Gabriel who was present at the house when the murder happened told the courtroom that he remembered his mother talking about killing his father a couple of days before the incident. But he didn't take her seriously because she would often speak nonsense.

On the other hand, Eli was devoted to Susan and was certain that she was not guilty at all. His story differed from everything the court heard from Adam and Gabriel because he presented his father as the one who abused the family. The way he spoke about Susan led the public to believe that their relationship was more complex. Some speculated that they were romantically involved but there was absolutely no evidence to support these claims.

Then the forensic experts took the stand. The prosecution presented the physical evidence found on Dr. Polk's body and they constructed the narrative that shed a light on everything that occurred on the night of the murder. It seemed like Susan entered the pool house from the kitchen, carrying the murder weapon, pepper spray, and a flashlight. Her intentions were clear – she wanted to cause harm to Felix Polk.

She confronted her husband who was getting ready for bed, used the pepper spray, and then hit his head with the flashlight. Once he was unconscious, Susan began stabbing him. The wounds were all over his body, including the chest, back, and even the feet. Each wound was pretty deep and caused damage to his internal organs. His lungs were torn and he was experiencing internal bleeding. It appeared that Felix did wake up during the attack because he had defensive wounds on his arms. However, his attempts failed because he was already fatally wounded. Susan did confirm that Felix tried to calm her down as she was delivering the blows, saying: "It is me! It is Felix!" He was convinced that Susan was in some sort of trance and he wanted her to snap back into the reality. He finally collapsed but he wasn't gone yet. As a matter of fact, Felix Polk slowly died on the floor of his pool house.

The investigators uncovered the fact that Susan tried to clean up the house after the murder. She exited the pool house, went into the kitchen, and washed off the blood from the knife. The murder weapon was then stored with the rest of the utensils like nothing had happened. Since the attack was very violent, Susan's clothes were covered in blood. She took everything off and turned on the washing machine. The murder happened late at night, so Susan listened to the sounds coming from the street. She was expecting the sirens because their neighbors lived very close to the pool house. But it seemed like nobody heard the struggle and commotion, or they simply brushed it off. There was only one thing she needed to do now, and that was to get rid of Felix's car. She waited for the morning to come, sat behind the wheel, and took his vehicle to the station. Felix was known to commute to his job, and Susan didn't want to risk her son seeing the car and asking questions.

These actions alone were enough to confirm that Susan knew what she had done and that there was no mental distress. Susan's self-defense story did not look good because she didn't have any wounds on her hands, which would occur if she tried to take away the blade from her husband. But this didn't stop her from hiring her own forensic pathologist to look into the case. Dr. John Cooper told the jury that Felix Polk was ill and had a heart condition. He supported Susan's defense by saying that the wounds would not kill Felix since he was very likely already dead from his heart disease. As a matter of fact, two of his main arteries were blocked and he suspected that Felix Polk's death was natural. However, Dr. Cooper failed to show up for cross-examination and didn't provide the judge with the documents which supported his claims. The forensic findings were not on Susan's side at all.

The trial ended on June 16th, 2006 when the jury reached the verdict – Susan Polk was guilty of a second-degree murder. She was sentenced to sixteen years to life. She looked like she expected that outcome and told the courtroom: "I won't be able to bake cookies, but maybe I'll write a couple of good stories." Paul Sequeira was relieved that the whole ordeal was over and gave the following statement to the media: "She's hateful. I have prosecuted many heinous criminals and she's not in that group, but I've never gone against anybody so hateful."

After the trial

Susan didn't want to give up so easily. She filed a motion for a new trial in 2007 because she felt like the jury was influenced by the media stories which were hard to avoid at the time. Almost all press accused Susan of the murder, and the jury knew that they would find her guilty even before the sentencing itself. Susan was also bothered by the fact that the jury consisted of women only, and assumed that they wanted to see her behind the bars.

She wasn't keen on the judge either, claiming that he didn't provide the jury with proper instructions, and forgot to mention that they have to stay away from the news outlets during the trial. But her motion was quickly denied since there wasn't enough evidence to support any of Susan's claims. She was taken back to prison to serve her time. She has been in California Institution for Women which is located in Corona, California since 2012 and will be eligible for a parole in 2017.

Prosecutor Paul Sequeira is certain that Susan will spend the rest of her life in prison. He said the following in 2006: "She will have to earn her way out and the chances of that are slim. She has no remorse. She is still defiant and I think she will be until she draws her last breath."

PSYCHO GIRL : THE TRUE STORY OF CATHERINE BIRNIE

39

JENA DICKENS

Catherine Margaret Harrison was born on May 23rd, 1951. Her partner, David John Birnie, was born on February 16th, 1951 and died on October 7th, 2015 by way of suicide. The duo was famously known throughout Australia as: The Killer Couple. They were from Perth, Australia and were found to have murdered four women ranging in age from 15 to 31 years old, over a span of about five weeks. Their fifth victim managed to escape through the bedroom window, while Catherine was distracted by a knock at the front door. The woman immediately ran and found help. The press referred to the heinous murders as the Moorhouse Murders. The victims were taken to Catherine and David's home located at 3 Moorhouse Street in Willagee, in Western Australia, a suburb of Perth.

Catherine was only two years old when her mother died in childbirth while giving birth to Catherine's younger brother. Her brother also died, two days later. Catherine's father, Harold, couldn't manage raising Catherine on his own at that time so she went to live with her maternal grandparents. When she was ten years old, Harold petitioned the court to receive custody of Catherine again, and he won. There always seemed to be a battle. Catherine's father didn't want her, but then wanted her, always back and forth. After Catherine was convicted of four counts of murder, it caused her father to suffer a nervous breakdown.

When Catherine was twelve years old she met a boy named David Birnie and they began dating two years later when they became teenagers. Both Catherine and David came from dysfunctional families. Their home life was chaotic and messy, literally as well as figuratively. David's mother was an alcoholic and his father was away at work the majority of the time. His father died in 1986 after battling a long illness. The house, as well as his mother, were messy and unkempt. She left her older children in charge of taking care of their younger siblings. She refused to do anything when it concerned the children and their welfare. Allegedly, David's mother would leave the refrigerator door open so that the children could eat throughout the day. David was the oldest of five children. David's school friends, as well as the local priest, deemed the family dysfunctional. The parents never prepared meals for their children, the house was always a mess, and the Priest, before marrying David's parents, said that he felt that their marriage would never lead to anything good. Little did he know how accurate his assumptions would be.

Catherine and David met through mutual friends shortly after David's family moved to the same Perth neighborhood as Catherine and her father. Catherine's father felt that David was trouble and a bad influence. Catherine had begun getting into a lot of trouble with the local police ever since the two of them met. Harold begged and pleaded with Catherine to stay away from David and stay out of trouble. Of course, this just brought the two closer. Whenever two kids are told not to do something, they go out of their way to blatantly disobey.

Even in adolescence David began exhibiting violent and perverse behavior. When David turned fifteen he dropped out of school and began working as jockey apprentice for Eric Parnham at the Ascot Race Course. While there, David would hurt the horses and also began his perverse career as an exhibitionist. David committed his first rape shortly after. By this point he had spent time in and out of jail for several charges ranging from misdemeanors to felonies. He built up a reputation around town as a sex and pornography addict.

Catherine was an accessory to a lot of crimes because of her involvement with David. They built up an extensive history of numerous charges including: breaking and entering, trespassing, unlawfully driving a motor vehicle, and theft. Catherine took the time, while in jail, to decide it was time to get away from David and start over. David had to serve a long jail sentence, while Catherine got off with probation. With the help of her parole officer, she found a job as a housekeeper working for the McLaughlin family. She ended up marrying the families' oldest son, Donald McLaughlin, on her twenty first birthday. They went on to have seven children. One of her children, however, was killed in a car accident while he was only an infant, leaving her with six of her children to take care of. Catherine was never really interested in motherhood though, and wasn't proud of her children and her family like another mother might be. She wasn't concerned about the children or keeping up with the house. Catherine was never truly happy. Her thoughts kept going back to her childhood love, David Birnie. The family that she had left never saw Catherine as a violent or evil person. Not unless she was around David.

Catherine finally reconnected with David Birnie after a thirteen year separation, four weeks after she gave birth to their seventh child. David had escaped from prison and the two of them had begun seeing each other. Catherine left her family and everything behind when David popped back into her life. They finally moved in together and Catherine had her last name changed to Birnie, although the couple never formally or legally got married. They moved into a white brick, two bedroom bungalow on Moorhouse Street. The house was unkempt, the property looked untended, and the house needed a fresh coat of paint. Catherine was completely dependent on David, emotionally and physically. Catherine was easily controlled and manipulated by David, and she would do anything and everything to make him happy. She never wanted to disappoint him. David had an insatiable sexual appetite and was said to have sex up to six times a day. He also accrued an extensive pornography collection and his brother claimed he always had someone. He always had a woman around. David's brother, James, had ended up staying with Catherine and David for a short while. James had just recently been released from prison after serving time for his own sex related offenses. He stayed with the couple for about six months. His brother went on to describe the numbing spray that David would spray on his penis before he had sex with all of the different women.

David and Catherine had exhausted all of their options sexually and began looking for new ways to pleasure themselves. They had spoken about abduction and rape, but had not realized that it would be just a few short weeks before they turned their fantasies into a heinous and perverted reality. Being as emotionally dependent on David as she was, it was easy for David to talk her into his abduction and rape plans. Catherine could never tell him no. She felt that she couldn't survive without him and would do anything to keep him. Catherine was completely codependent and David always seemed to be in control. She wanted David to have all the pleasure and excitement that he wanted but knew that they had exhausted all efforts between just the two of them.

The abductions, rapes, and brutal murders began on October 6th, 1986. The couple didn't really care who their victims were, as long as they were female and alone. Twenty two year old Mary Neilson arrived at the Moorhouse Street residence to inquire about some tires that David had for sale. Mary was a student at the University of Western Australia where she was pursuing her degree in Psychology. Once inside the house, David took Mary by knife point and chained her to their bed and gagged her. Catherine stood in the room and watched as David raped the girl repeatedly. After the rape, the couple took Mary to Gleneagles National Park. David raped her one more time and then strangled her with a nylon cord and stabbed her through the heart. The couple then buried Mary in a shallow grave. Catherine looked on while David committed these violent acts, however, she did not yet participate.

The second murder took place on October 20th. The victim was fifteen year old, Susannah Candy. Susannah was a high school student attending Hollywood High School. She lived with her parents and had two brothers and one sister. Catherine and David Birnie had been driving around for several hours that night in search of their next victim. The couple finally found a girl walking along Stirling Highway, by herself, trying to hitch a ride. As soon as she got into David's car she had a knife to her throat and she was taken to the Birnies' home. While at the home, she was forced to write letters to her family explaining that she decided to run away. David repeatedly raped Susannah while she lay bound and gagged. Catherine had gotten into the bed with them and tried to strangle her with the nylon cord, but Susannah began fighting back. They forced sleeping pills down her throat, and once she passed out they successfully strangled her with the cord. The couple took Susannah to the State Park and buried her in a shallow grave, like their previous victims. This was the first time that Catherine took part in the murder. Catherine never showed any form of remorse over what she had done. When later asked why she contributed she said, "I wanted to see how strong I was within my inner self. I didn't feel a thing. It was like I expected. I was prepared to follow him to the end of the earth and do anything to see that his desires were satisfied. She was a female. Females hurt and destroy males."

On November 1st, the Killer Couple comes across their third victim, Noelene Patterson. Noelene was on her way home from work when her car ran out of gas. Noelene was a bar manager and had been working at Nedland's Golf Club that day. She was standing beside her car when David pulled up to her and offered his help. The thirty one year old got into David's car and was immediately met with a knife at her throat. She was taken to Moorhouse Street where she was bound and gagged, while being raped repeatedly. The original plan, like the others, was to kill the girl that same night. David had seemed to develop feelings for Noelene however. Catherine noticed the fondness that David had for the woman and became extremely jealous and increasingly upset. Noelene represented the type of person that Catherine could only wish to be and she absolutely despised her because of this. Catherine gave David an ultimatum at this point. She put the knife to her own chest and said, 'you either kill her tonight, or I will kill myself.' It was on the third night, after being given the ultimatum, that David gave Noelene several sleeping pills and then strangled her. She was then taken to the park and buried beside the other victims. Catherine admitted to taking pleasure in throwing sand in the victims face as David coldly buried her with no remorse.

Catherine and David's fourth victim, Denise Brown, suffered the same fate as the previous women who had the unfortunate experience of crossing paths with the Killer Couple. Denise Brown was twenty one years old, and was taken on November 5, 1986 while waiting at a bus stop. She was gagged and raped repeatedly before being put into the car and taken to Pine Plantation, where she was raped again while David waited for a blanket of darkness to fall. After it got dark he took her out and raped her again, while stabbing her in the neck. As David began burying her, thinking she was dead, Denise surprised the couple by sitting straight up in her grave. David struck her in the head twice with an axe as Catherine looked on in shock and amazement. David has said that he learned bodies would decompose at a faster rate if you stabbed them.

Detective Sergeant Paul Ferguson was the first to realize that he could be dealing with a serial killer, after the fourth woman was reported missing. Years later he recalled his experience while working on the case. He recalls how this case still haunts him and when asked why replied, "Because it was the most interesting and horrific I've had in my career," and "I have things tucked away back here that I pray to God I never pull out of the drawer." All of the missing women had come from relatively good homes and they never got into any real trouble. Their families found the phone calls and letters they received very suspicious.

The couples' fifth and final victim was seventeen year old Kate Moir. She was on her way home, after a night out with her friends, when she was abducted by the couple. The date of this final abduction was November 10th, 1986. Kate was the only one of their victims that was able to escape and run and find help. David had left the house for work that day. Catherine was home with Kate. She forced her to call her parents and tell them that she would be staying at a friend's house. When Catherine heard a knock at the door, she left Kate alone, untied, and went to see who was there. Kate took the opportunity to escape through the open window and ran half naked to the nearest store. She ran in crying and pleading for help. Kate was taken to the Palmyra police station and questioned. She was able to give the police a full description of Catherine and David, as well as inform the police of the couples' address. After their arrest, Catherine admitted to knowing Kate, but the couple said that the sexual acts were consensual and she was a willing participant. The police performed a search of the Birnie's home and found Kate's bag, as well as a pack of cigarettes that Kate had managed to hide in the ceiling in order to prove that she was there. After hours of questioning, Catherine and David finally admitted to the rape and murders of the four women and agreed to show the police where they had buried them. Three of the victims had been buried in Gleneagle State Forest and one on the Pine Plantation. The couple showed no emotion, whatsoever, as the police dug up the graves. David was the one who showed the police the locations of the women, except for one. Catherine insisted that she be the one to show them where Noelene was buried. She showed no regret, only anger. She spat on Noelene's grave and made her strong feelings of hate toward her very vocal to the detective. She explained to the police, in great detail, how much she despised Noelene Patterson. As they were leaving, David turned to Detective Katich and said chillingly, "What a pointless loss of young life." They showed absolutely no remorse for what they had done. This statement stuck with the detectives for years to follow. They couldn't believe how little the couple seemed to care or regret what they had been done. In some ways, however, they thought Catherine was relieved that it was finally over.

Catherine admitted to not caring about participating in the rapes and murders of the women, until they got to Denise Brown. "I think

I must have come to a decision that sooner or later there had to be an end to the rampage. I had reached the stage when I didn't know what to do. I suppose I came to a decision that I was prepared to give her a chance." The brutal manner in which Denise was murdered seemed to hit Catherine hard. She witnessed David not only stab her repeatedly but strike her in the head with the axe. "Deep and dark in the back of my mind was yet another fear. I had a great fear that I would have to look at another killing like that of Denise Brown, the girl he murdered with the axe."

In response to Kate Moir's escape, due to Catherine's carelessness with her victim, she said, "I knew that it was a foregone conclusion that David would kill her, and probably do it that night. I was just fed up with the killings. I thought if something did not happen soon it would simply go on and on and never end."

Kate Moir survived the abduction and attacks of Australia's most infamous serial killers. Instead of remaining a victim, she chose to be a survivor. She also sought to seek reform for the way her government handled cases like hers.

"I want to see no parole for wilful murder. I want a reintroduction of wilful murder as a charge. I want truth in sentencing. I want no parole for sex offenders and child sex offenders. We have been softening our justice system for years."

Kate Moir is a married woman and mother of three children. She constantly fights for the changes and justice she deserves. The following are quotes that were made by Kate, again concerning Catherine's parole and the possibility of her release.

"I want the legacy that I leave to be that of a survivor and a hero, not a victim. But enough is enough."

"I want the Attorney General to change the law and stop reviewing Catherine Birnie's parole. She does not apply for it herself, it is automatically reviewed and every time it happens, it causes me incredible pain."

"Every time I hear that her parole is being reviewed, I relive the nightmare. It causes significant trauma because I relive it and it feels like it happened yesterday. My name was always protected because I was a minor at the time I was captured, but due to the internet, if anybody googles my name it is everywhere and linked to the Birnie killings."

The couple appeared in court on November 12th, 1986. This was just two days after their fifth victim had escaped and they were arrested. The court proceedings took place at Fremantle Magistrates Court. They both refused any kind of representation, no plea was entered, bail was refused, and they were remanded into custody. Catherine allegedly took photos and the couple also recorded video of their criminal acts. At trial, the police were in possession of the video evidence. On February 10, 1987 a crowd gathered outside of the courthouse. When they saw the couple being ushered in for trial they screamed and chanted, "Hang the Bastards!" The community was outraged over the news of the serial killings that took place and wanted David and Catherine to receive the maximum sentence. They even wanted to reinstate the death penalty for David and Catherine Birnie.

Bill Power, the court reporter, spoke about the proceedings and the manners in which the couple acted while in court. He said that it would be something that would always stick with him, he would never forget.

"There was nothing distinctive about David and Catherine when they first appeared in court to face multiple murder charges in the serial killings which brought an end to the mystery of young women going missing off Perth streets."

"They were a rather nondescript, ordinary looking couple you might find running a petrol station in a country town. David was a weedy little man and Catherine his drab, slightly buxom wife with a very sour face. Both were accompanied by male police officers."

"If you have ever witnessed a wild cat go off, then try and imagine some hellcat in the confined spaces of a narrow staircase. Catherine Birnie fought against the guarding police officers and refused to allow any of them

to touch her as she screamed and spat her words at them until she reached the dock and spotted her beloved, David. Only then did she calm down."

It had also been said previously, by some people in the community that the couple never looked like the type that could commit such violent acts. They looked like normal and ordinary people. But the secret horrors of what occurred in their home on Moorhouse Street would paint a very different image of the couple.

Trial Judge Justice Wallace said in trial, "Each of these horrible crimes were premeditated, planned, and carried out cruelly and relentlessly over a comparatively short period."

Right before Judge Wallace sentenced Catherine, he delivered the following message to her. He explained that he did not believe that even though she pled guilty, that she was truly sorry for what she had done. She had pled guilty and avoided a long trial, and spared the victims' families from having to relive over and over what happened to their loved ones, but she showed no remorse, no emotion, no sympathy for the crimes she had committed with David Birnie.

"You willingly joined in the selection of your unfortunate victims, carried them off at knifepoint, and held them in captivity for the sole purpose of the sexual gratification of your partner in crime and then murdered them, lest you be identified, and then finally mutilated them. You personally extinguished the life of two of your victims and certainly participated in the death of the third. The only appropriate punishment is the sentence I intend to impose, strict life security in prison."

Remember, Catherine was completely devoted, obsessed, and brainwashed when it came to David. She would do anything and everything for him to make sure he was happy. This is the driving factor that David used to manipulate and control her. He needed an accomplice and she was more than willing, and he knew it. Catherine and David received four separate life sentences for the abduction, torture, rape, and murder of Mary Neilson, Susannah Candy, Noelene Patterson, and Denise Brown. Under sentencing laws, their case was brought up every three years automatically for parole. Kate began a crusade to ensure that the couple remained in prison. She grew a social media presence and page entitled, We Support Kate, as well as worked with the Empowerment Foundation in an attempt to build an online reform petition. Kate also received support from Catherine's son, Peter. He chose not to release his surname to the public, due to the physical and emotional abuse he has been forced to face in relation to his mother's crimes. He had suffered personal and professional ruin, as soon as people learned about his family history. He had been turned down for jobs, lost jobs he had, and even lost his fiancé because of his family background. Peter was only five years old when his mother was arrested. He saw his mother on television because of it shortly after her arrest. When speaking out on the abuse he faced, he recalled horrible stories of what happened to him, and his siblings, while growing up. He also stated that the mandatory parole hearings, every three years, prevented him from getting on with his life. Having to hear about his mother and relive the violence his mother was responsible for every few years, was an interruption to his life, and it made it harder to maintain a sense of normalcy within his career life and personal life. In an interview with the West Australian, Peter stated, "I want the parole board to hear I don't want her out. I don't want to see her out." He also said, "I have had baseball bats to the head, I have been jumped on and kicked at. I have been knocked out."

After pleading guilty and receiving their sentences, David was initially sent to maximum security Fremantle Prison, he was eventually moved into solitary confinement. He did not get along with the other prisoners and was constantly getting into fights. The inmates frequently and violently attacked David. A day before he was due in trial for the charge of rape of an inmate, David hung himself in his jail cell. His suicide occurred in 2009 at Casuarina Prison. Catherine's request to attend David's funeral was refused.

Catherine was sent to Bandyup Women's prison where she was eventually employed as the head librarian. While in prison, the couple exchanged over 2600 letters, but were denied any other form of contact. Catherine's mandatory parole hearings were finally revoked in 2009, and her papers were subsequently marked: 'never to be released.'

While many people are against Catherine Birnie ever getting parole, one man stands against this argument. Perth QC Tom Percy disagrees with the opinion of people that had been saying that some people just don't deserve a second chance. The following quotes by Percy outline his argument of Catherine not remaining in prison and the likelihood of her harming the community, as well as his stance of being in favor of Catherine's parole.

"She should not be kept in prison to satisfy society's thirst for revenge."

"She has been there thirty odd years and you would think it might be time for us to say she has done her time. She has done her statutory minimum prescribed by the court, which was in possession of all of the facts."

"I am not sure she could really be a threat to anyone anymore, and all my information from Bandyup Womens' Prison is that she is a little old granny that goes about her work in the library like a church mouse."

"This case just so happened to be one that caught the public attention, even though she was not the prime mover in it. David is now dead."

"What's the point of keeping her in there? Sadly, it looks like she will never get parole, but I think she probably deserves it."

Despite his argument and fight to get Catherine released from prison, she still remains behind bars. She has not requested any new parole hearings, herself, as of yet. Some people in the community had gone as far as to say that if she were to be released, then maybe Percy should allow her to live with him in his residence.

It was now January of 1987. A letter written by Catherine Birnie, while in prison, eventually surfaced. It was a letter she had written to her six children in an attempt to explain some of her actions that led to her being placed in prison and why she left them in the first place. The letter reads as followed:

"Dear kids, Hi! Mum here...the reason I changed my name to Birnie was so that you kids wouldn't be hurt by the newspapers and television people. I am not proud of what has been said about me, but I have to live with that and the memories. As to why this happened, I can only hope that the doctors can help me to find out.....I never stopped loving any of you kids. Maybe I was wrong about leaving you but I thought you would be safer with your father."

Catherine's husband, Donald, claimed that he had still wanted her back. This was after trial and after he heard of the horrific acts she had committed with David. He stated, 'you can't stop loving someone after fifteen years of marriage.' Donald's mother stood firmly beside her son, saying that Catherine had been good and non-violent, until David cast his spell over her. Catherine's nephew, Leonard Nock, stood beside his aunt claiming, "All Aunt Cathy wanted was someone to lean on. She never had a mother. She is a very caring person. She and I are very close. I used to call her my mum. She was never the violent type, she never used to hit the kids. It is not the Cathy we used to know and love." In Catherine's letter she also persuaded the children to tell their father to divorce her. She said their father needed to move on and this was the way it needed to be done. She didn't hold out any hope for her eventual release and didn't want Donald to wait for her, because it was never going to happen. She also asked the children to get permission from Donald to write back to her, and maybe even one day go and visit her. The family put the entirety of the blame on David. They refused to admit to or believe that Catherine had anything to do with the violence. During their prison visits, the family also failed to even ask Catherine the question regarding her guilt or innocence. They didn't want to hear the answer, therefore, they never even asked the question.

Catherine Bernie was up for parole in 2013 and again in 2016. She was denied both years. She is once again up for review sometime in 2019. "Now barring any reason to keep her in, and revenge I don't consider enough of a reason. She should be released."-Percy

Despite Percy's statements, Catherine Birnie remains in prison to this very day, with little to no chance of parole. People, even to this day, wonder if the abductions, the perverse rape, and heinous murders would have continued long past the few weeks they had gotten away with it. If they had never been caught, would they have continued? Finally, were there other victims that they never confessed to? Other gravesites that have yet to be located? It is too late for David Birnie to tell anyone, but Catherine still has the chance to admit to any other wrongdoing she had done before her permanent home in prison forced her to keep distance between herself and her lover. I guess we will never know.

"I honestly believe that woman has never given those victims one ounce of consideration, both the dead victims and the families of the victims...They [David and Catherine Birnie] were parasites who lived off of each other. The most evil people I have ever, ever come across."-Detective Paul Ferguson.

SERIAL KILLING MOM : THE TRUE STORY OF JANIE LOU GIBBS

54

JANE CARLISLE

Janie Lou Hickox was born on December 25th, Christmas day, 1932 in Cordele, Georgia. Cordele is now a town with just over 11 000 residents, and is proudly known as the Watermelon Capital of the World. The city is named after Cordelia Hawkins who was the eldest daughter of Colonel Samuel Hawkins, the president of the Savannah, Americus and Montgomery Railway. In November of 1864, the area temporarily served as the capital of Georgia, but Cordele as it is now knows was founded in 1888 as a junction between two major railroads: the Savannah, Americus and Montgomery line and the Georgia Southern and Florida. Notable people from the area include jazz and blues singers, sportsmen, a White House Press Secretary and the president of an international Christian TV network. Nobody suspected that a serial killer who would be a black widow was growing up in their midst.

There is not much information about Janie's upbringing, but it was strictly religious and she grew up in a fairly poor family. Janie was married to Charles Clayton Gibbs, a farmer, when she was only fifteen. The two moved to the nearby town of Arabi which was just under ten miles away from Cordele, a mere fifteen minutes by car. Both of these towns fall under the Crisp County district. Arabi now has a population of 586, with 185 hosueholds and 125 families living in the town. Janie and Charles were regular churchgoers, and they had three boys: Roger Ludean Gibbs, Melvin Watess Gibbs, and Marvin Ronald Gibbs. For eighteen years, they lived quiet and devoted lives on the farm until tragedy began to take blow after blow upon the family.

Janie was known for spending all of her spare time helping out at the church and for her day-care service that she ran in her home for children of working mothers. Accounts note that on most days Janie would have around twenty-five children at her house aside from her own sons. While some believed her to have almost fanatic religious beliefs, all members of Janie's church and community believed her to be sound of mind and to know the difference between right and wrong, testimonies that they would later make in the investigation. Nobody felt that Janie had any emotional or mental issues, and simply knew her as a devoted mother who held God and the church close to her heart. When she wasn't looking after children in the community, Janie was helping out with events around the church and other ways to support the congregation.

Just before the tragedies began to occur, Janie had travelled to Albany, Georgia for a doctor's appointment. There she had been diagnosed with Lou Gehrig's disease, a motor neurone disease that destroys muscle control, is also known as amyotrophic lateral sclerosis or ALS. The disease progresses from a stiffness of muscles to twitching while the person becomes increasingly weaker. Eventually, once their muscles have decreased in size enough, the patient has trouble with speaking, swallowing, and eventually breathing. Janie was very aware that her body would begin to systematically shut itself down. After her trial, her defense lawyer Frank Martin stated that this was one of the most tragic aspects of the case as far as he was concerned. Frank believed that due to Janie's acute awareness of how her illness would progress paired with her fanatic religious beliefs, she wanted everybody that was close to her in the world to go to heaven so that she would be with them when she finally passed. Although Janie never admitted this in court, the murder of her husband, three sons, and grandson, all of whom she loved dearly, suggests that this might have been a contributing factor to the decisions or delirium that ended in her intentionally poisoning five members of her family.

The first member of the family to go was her husband, Charles Clayton Gibbs, who died on the 21st January 1966 when he was only thirty-nine years old. Janie was an avid cook, and she always had home cooked meals ready for her family when they returned home from work or school. After having had one such meal, Charles collapsed in the family home and was taken to hospital. Janie went to the hospital to care for him and brought a flask of soup with her. After Charles was served this final meal, he died painfully from stomach cramps and convulsions. Years later, investigators realized that this soup must have been laced with a particularly strong dose of arsenic from rat poison that Janie had been giving him in trace amount in his meals and coffees.

When administered in small amounts like this, it can be very difficult to determine if somebody is a victim of arsenic poisoning unless a doctor thinks to specifically check for it. Arsenic poisoning can result in a host of different symptoms and organ failures, so it is often the case that medical professionals are waiting for more evidence to be able to provide a solid diagnosis while the victim continues to be poisoned by somebody close to them. Symptoms can include abdominal pain and cramping, diarrhea, vomiting, dark urine, dehydration, vertigo, delirium, shock, hair loss, and convulsions. Arsenic is flavorless and odorless, making it very difficult for somebody to connect their normal food and beverage consumption with their illness. Arsenic poisoning can affect the skin, liver, lungs, and kidneys, which is both why it is such a potentially fatal condition and why it is difficult to detect without a hunch. In the case of Charles, his death was written down to an undiagnosed liver disease that he had been suffering for some time. While the doctors wanted to perform an autopsy on her husband to be sure, Janie said that she didn't want him 'all cut up', and her wishes were respected.

The church community provided an overwhelming amount of support for the Gibbs family once Charles had passed. The entire congregation was shocked, Charles having seemed to be in such good health until recent times, and also because he was still so young. The Gibbs family were provided with company, meals, emotional support, and everything that the members of their church community could possibly extend. When the life insurance claim for Charles came through, Janie donated a significant portion of these funds to the church to demonstrate her thanks for everything that they had done and her belief in the community. Janie claimed that she and the boys would have to continue on as best they could, and that she felt that with the strength of the church community behind them they would be able to make it through. Even after their home burned down soon after Charles' death and the family moved back to Janie's home town of Cordele, Janie continued to offer day-care services for the children of working mothers. There has never been an investigation into the house burning down, but the timing is certainly curious. Is it possible that Janie felt this was the only way to justify moving her family back to her home town of Cordele? It is clear from the rest of her actions over this two year period that she wasn't thinking rationally, and perhaps she wanted to escape the physical environment where she had been married for all of those years. Whatever the reason, just as nobody suspected that Janie had anything to do with the death of her husband, there was no investigation into whether or not the house burned down due to arson.

It was around this time that the oldest Gibbs son Roger took notice of a girl in their congregation, Ellen Penny. A relationship began to blossom between them under the watchful eye of Janie. The two teenagers began to spend more and more time together at church events, and participated in the same activities together. If Roger was assigned the duty of retrieving the bibles at the end of a ceremony, Ellen would always be there too help him. Very soon the two began to date. Over the next year Roger and Ellen married and she became pregnant with their first child. Ellen began living at the Gibb's residence, but this relationship and pregnancy was against a dark backdrop. It is difficult to say whether Janie took an immediate dislike to Ellen, or whether she did not want her son getting married and having a child so early like she had herself. Perhaps she wanted a different life for him, or harbored some resentment on being married off at such a young age. Either way, Janie never had a good relationship with Ellen and many times would behave as if she almost didn't register her existence.

Only months after Charles' death, Marvin began to develop the same symptoms as his father had. Having moved house and town, perhaps the rest of the family felt a separation with losing their father and like this wouldn't happen again with their youngest brother. There are no records of comments from the brothers or the community being concerned that Marvin would go the same way as his father, but sure enough, nine months after his father had died, Marvin Ronald Gibbs died on the 29th August 1966. Marvin too was determined to have an undiagnosed liver disease just like his father had, and Janie once again refused to have an autopsy performed. Perhaps Janie felt that performing an autopsy was an ungodly act that would in some way affect the chances of her family members getting into heaven? While the largest reason was most certainly to protect her own interests and for her to be able to complete her task, autopsy is a process rejected by many faiths and traditions. The police and staff at the insurance company pushed for autopsies as they felt that two deaths of this nature so close together and in one family didn't make sense. At this time, some members of the church community began to have suspicions about the deaths in the Gibbs family, but nobody wanted to be the one to come forward and accuse the pious and highly involved church member that Janie was. For many, there was still a huge disconnect. So even though the insurance company and the police of Crisp County were pressing for an autopsy on the body of young Marvin, Janie still had the support of the community enough to request that this procedure not be undertaken. Despite their suspicions, many in the community still felt that Janie wouldn't be capable of doing such a thing, particularly when it was to her own family that she seemed to have such an active devotion to.

Once again the church community poured support for the Gibb's family, offering counsel and companionship for Janie and her two remaining boys. When Marvin's life insurance came through, Janie once again provided a large portion of this claim to the church, which was undergoing significant renovations. While some began to talk about Janie seeming to almost be enjoying her new lifestyle, never being seen in the same dress and buying a new car, they could not help notice how generous she was also being with these funds. Those members of the community who still had faith in Janie chalked this spending down to a way to cope with her losses. However, Ellen Penny remained highly suspicious of Janie Gibbs. She didn't know how to speak out about her, both because she needed to live with the family and because she was so young, but after Marvin's death Ellen was certain that what was happening to the Gibbs family was no random or hereditary tragedy. Then, Melvin also began to fall ill.

As Melvin (often referred to in some articles as Lester) began to follow the path of his father and younger brother, the sixteen year old started to experience dizzy spells. Some people in the community attributed these headaches to puberty as the boy was sixteen. By this point, with such serious difficulties in the family, it is a wonder that Melvin's complaints weren't taken more seriously. He went downhill sharply. The doctors, not wanting to claim his death as another bout of undiagnosed liver disease that they weren't certain of, labeled his death a result of hepatitis. Once again a claim was made for life insurance, a portion donated to the church, and support lavished upon the Gibbs' family. At this point, Ellen became terrified for the life of her husband, herself, and their unborn child.

About a month after Melvin's death, Ellen and Roger's baby, Raymond, was born. Everybody noticed that Janie's mood lifted, and the community felt that this is where the horror ended for the Gibb's family. Janie was thrilled with her grandson, even though she had been so early married herself and her son had had his first child so early, making Janie a grandmother at thirty-four. Janie often used to show the baby to anybody who came around to the house, and would often be seen out with Raymond around the city. Ellen began to feel at ease around this time as Janie seemed to have changed entirely. The way that she interacted with Ellen seemed to have improved, and it seemed that the way that Janie went about all of her daily tasks with a different air.

However, even the baby began to fall ill soon. Ellen was in a state of desperation and didn't know what to do, the child only being one month old. The young girl has nobody that she could turn to, and didn't feel confident enough to make an accusation against Janie, even to her own husband. Despite the fact that Raymond was perfectly healthy, he died of an apparent heart condition. Everybody who was close to the Gibbs were completely shocked to hear of Raymond's death, and this is the point that many members of the congregation became highly suspicious of Janie. However, nobody did anything to prevent her from claiming the fifth and final member of her immediate family, her eldest and grieving son, with both Roger and Ellen still living with her at the time.

In the weeks after their baby died, Roger began to fall ill. Ellen, who was still under twenty at this age, had still not found the courage or the means to speak out against Janie. This may have been due to her living situation, or perhaps due to the sudden death of her son, but as Roger grew increasingly ill Ellen could do nothing but watch him deteriorate. She notes that during this time her husband constantly had red eyes, had visible rings around these, and was always pale and lacking in energy. He also used to get very severe headaches, but wasn't the type of person that liked to talk about any suffering that he was experiencing. The most that he would discuss these headaches was when he would be in such pain that he would be flinching. Ellen would ask if his head was giving him trouble again, to which he would respond with short and basic answers. Roger eventually found himself bedridden, being cared for by his mother. Despite what had happened to his father, two brothers, and own son, Roger never shared any suspicions about his mother with Ellen. It is entirely possible that he had figured out what was going on, being the last left, but didn't know how to get himself out of the situation.

Over the weeks, Roger's health got worse and worse. Ellen remembers overhearing an argument between Roger and his mother where he was repeatedly saying

"You did it! You did this to me!"

He was saying it over and over again as fiercely as he was able to in his deteriorated state. Ellen did not fully understand the conversation as she made sure that she kept out of sight. She asked Roger about it later in private, but he didn't reveal anything further and simply said that he and his mother had been squabbling over something. Ellen began to wonder whether she was paranoid about the situation, but it seemed that everything was pointing towards Janie's involvement in not only Roger's sickness but the suspicious deaths of the other four. Ellen stayed by her husband and cared for him as best she could, watching on as Janie nursed her son.

When Roger was eventually placed in hospital, Janie and Ellen spent nearly all of their time there. After a couple of days, Ellen noticed that Janie was in the habit of taking the water jug that the hospital placed in their room, tipping it down the sink, and replacing it with her own water. When Ellen asked her why she was doing this, Janie claimed that the hospital water had too much sulfur and that it hurt his throat. It was later realized that she was feeding her last remaining immediate family member increasing doses of arsenic through the water. Janie forced Roger to drink the water in large gulps and often. Once again, it is difficult to understand why this behavior was accepted by nurses, and also why nobody gave Roger testing for arsenic poisoning when four members of his family had died so suspiciously. However, even though this was a fairly common way for women to kill at the time, it is not until later years that we realized the signs and hints that might have saved the Gibbs family from their wife and mother.

One day, Janie asked Ellen to give Roger some water. Janie filled up a tall glass and placed it in Ellen's hand. Ellen gave Roger a small sip, but Janie demanded that he finish the whole glass, telling her that his throat is dry and he needs more. Ellen tipped the whole glass of water down her husband's throat, unknowingly giving him the final and strongest dose of arsenic. Perhaps Janie had been hoping that the blame might be placed on Ellen, or maybe she got satisfaction out of Ellen being the one that finally killed Roger, Janie having never been too keen on the girl. As Janie didn't want an autopsy on Roger, just like it was for the others, it is hard to say whether this act was a final insurance in her mind of her not being guilty of the crime, or whether it was the latter and she got satisfaction out of Ellen killing her spouse unintentionally. It is also possible, with Roger being left for last, that she was the least willing to kill him and needed Ellen to perform this final duty. After all, it would have made sense to kill the older two sons first and leave the younger one in her care, Marvin being so young and the least able of all three brothers to be able to take any action against his mother even if he had figured out what was happening. This suggests that Roger might have been somewhat of a favorite of Janie's, and that she wanted as much time with him as she could. Whatever the reason, Roger died soon after receiving the dose. He was only nineteen, and this finished Janie's work, whether it was insurance fraud or what she perceived to be God's work.

Just as she had with her two younger sons and her husband, Janie attempted to stop medical professionals from undertaking autopsies on Roger and Raymond Gibbs. However, as Ellen was the wife and mother, she has the rights of next of kin. Autopsies were performed that revealed extremely high levels of arsenic in Roger's organs, around twenty times that which you would expect to find in a body during an autopsy where arsenic has not been the cause of death. It was at this time that the Crisp County police called for the bodies of Charles, Marvin, and Melvin to be exhumed. People crowded around at the graveyard to watch while the bodies were taken out of the ground and placed on blue tarps. People began to say that they had thought there was something suspicious the whole time. A lot of guilt began to spread through the community. What if they had mentioned something earlier? Would they have at least been able to save the lives of Roger and his infant son? Mothers who had given their children to Janie to look after day in and day out felt embarrassed about their judgment of her character. This time the sympathy poured out for young Ellen who has lost her home, husband, and baby all within the space of a month. All five murders were committed in a short period of time, between 1966 and 1967. In all, Janie had received $31 000 in life insurance payments and given around ten percent of this to the church, but now she would have to answer for the crimes that she had done against those in the world that trusted her the most. Eric Hickey who has performed a study on female serial killers including Janie Lou Gibbs in 1991 claims that "These are the *quiet killers*, every bit as lethal as male serial murderers, but we are seldom aware of one in our midst because of their low visibility." Hickey also found that it takes an average of eight years to catch a female serial killer, nearly double what it takes on average to identify and arrest male serial killers.

Janie was arrested on Christmas Eve 1967, the day before her thirty-fifth birthday. She admitted to having killed all five of her immediate family members, but claimed that she didn't have a motive for doing so. While many people claim that she did this for the insurance money, there is still the chance that she genuinely committed the crimes in the name of her fanatic religious beliefs, wanting her family to be with her in heaven.

By February, Janie was determined to be insane and not fit for a trial but it was still agreed that she should not be able to live out her life in the community as she had been before. Janie took up residence at a state mental hospital where she served as a hospital cook, living there until 1976. At this time, multiple people had testified that they thought Janie was aware enough of her actions that she should have to deal with their legal ramifications. On May 9th 1976, Janie was convicted for her crimes and handed down five life sentences, one for each family member that she had poisoned. Janie's sister came to visit her in an attempt to understand the things that Janie has done, but found that she was largely nonresponsive and bewildered. The first question that her sister asked was *Why did you kill your family, Janie?* To which Janie responded she didn't know. Her sister attempted again, saying *Do you feel guilty?* Janice once again responded that she didn't know, seeming to be removed and numbed to the situation. Her sister made one final attempt to reach out to Janie and understand what had happened, asking *Can I do anything to help you?* For the third time, Janie responded that she didn't know. Her sister continued to visit her in jail in an attempt to understand more about Janie, what she had done, and what she was going through. But it seemed that no matter how much she tried, Janie was like a shell of what she had previously been.

She came up for parole seventeen times but was denied on each occasion. In April of 1999, due to her failing health as a result of Parkinson's disease, Janie was released into her sister's care. The last years of her life were spent in a wheel chair at a nursing home in Douglasville, Georgia, where she died on February 7th 2010. She now rests in the Sunrise Memorial Gardens at Lithia Springs in Douglas County, Georgia.

SERIAL KILLING MOM : THE TRUE STORY OF STACEY CASTOR

PAULA ANTHONY

Stacey Ruth Castor may have been one of the most sociopathic female serial killers in modern times. She poisoned her first husband Michael Wallace with anti-freeze after he becomes an inconvenience to her and did the same to her second husband David Castor years later. When she caught wind that the police were onto her methods, she poisoned her own daughter and wrote 'confession' letter on her behalf.

She tried to pin the crimes on her daughter.

Dubbed the Black Widow by the national media, recent findings have opened up the possibility that Stacey killed her own father as well.

Cool, calm and collected, Stacey maintained her innocence throughout the court proceedings, adamantly pointing the finger of blame at her own daughter. But what possessed her to kill not only her husbands but her own flesh and blood?

This is her story.

EARLY LIFE

Stacey was born July 27th, 1967 in Clay, New York. She would meet what she called the 'love of her life' in a bar at age seventeen.

His name was Michael Wallace.

"There was some kind of bet going on," Stacey's daughter, Ashley Wallace said. "He (Michael) had bet a friend that he would take her home that night. Then after that night they were together."

Stacey stated that she knew within the first five minutes of meeting Michael that she would marry him.

Michael was six years older than Stacey. He was loud and gregarious, always laughing and looking for a good time. This was a contrast to the personality of Stacey who was more withdrawn and kept people at arm's length. Michael brought her out of her shell.

"He was like something out of the 'Dukes of Hazzard'," Michael's brother-in-law Jonathon Corbett said. "He was all about yee-haw! Let's go have a beer. Just for fun. Let's go for a ride. Just for fun."

It would take five years for the couple to marry as they tied the knot at Stacey's parent's home.

Michael was a happy go lucky guy. But this happiness was fueled by drugs and alcohol according to Stacey.

"He had a problem with both for a long time in his life," Stacey recalled.

Michael would be arrested on numerous occasions for DUI. Finally, the judge got fed up and sent him to jail for a short period of time.

After he got out of jail, Michael vowed to change his ways. The couple married and Stacey would give birth to their first daughter, Ashley, in 1988.

"I knew from that minute on, my whole reason for being here was to take care of her," Stacey said.

Three years later, they would welcome another daughter, Bree.

Stacey would work as a dispatcher for an ambulance company while Michael worked nights as a mechanic. Times were hard financially but their contrast in personalities look to do them in. They would fight but it would not be about money because according to Stacey, "they had none."

PARENTAL FAVORITISM

Among their many disputes, Stacey would accuse Michael of favoring the youngest daughter Bree over everyone else. He would call Bree his "little princess" while paying less attention to Ashley. Stacey said that she made up for this perceived favoritism by becoming closer to Ashley.

"Bree was daddy's little angel," Stacey's friend Dani Colman said. "She could do no wrong. There was no talk of any relationship between Ashley and Michael Wallace."

The couple would continue to grow apart over the years and each was rumored to have had affairs. Still, their weakening marriage didn't seem to affect the children as both daughters remembered their childhood with a fondness.

"We'd just go for a ride in the car, you know?" Bree said. "For no reason, just take a ride. That was fun."

But by 1999, the couple were at odds on a daily basis. Suddenly, Michael began feeling sick. Over the holidays, his family members would describe him as having an unsteady gait and looking bloated. More than one person suggested that he see a doctor.

Michael would die in early 2000 with only eleven-year-old Ashley present in the room. She noticed he was sick but didn't think to call the doctor.

"He was laying on the couch, making what I thought were funny faces," Ashley said. "And all of sudden, he just sticks his arm up in the air and puts his arm on his side and then his arm just fell down."

Ashley left her father on the couch and went to pick up her sister Bree from school. "I've relived this day over and over again in my head, because what if there was something that I could've done?" Ashley recalled . "Like, I should've known, but I didn't. I was 11!"

Doctors would tell Stacey that Michael died of a heart attack. Michael's sister, however, held her suspicions about his demise.

"The color of his skin from head to chest was deep, dark purple," Michael's sister, Rosemary Corbett said. And it was really weird."

She wanted an autopsy but Stacey steadfastly refused.

"Stacey knew how to cover her tracks," forensic psychiatrist Paula Orange said. "Her mistakes came later in her serial killer career. And she was a serial killer, make no mistake about that. She didn't kill so much for profit or money. She killed out of convenience. When something wasn't going her way and she had to eliminate someone, she would do it without remorse or feeling."

THE GRIEVING PROCESS

Stacey took her two daughters and did her best to try and move on with their lives. She treated the girls to a trip to Disney World to try and put some happiness back in their life. Her gestures seemed empty to the children as she continued to hold things in and became colder to her children.

"My mom was never really around (after Michael died)," Ashley said. "I did all of the things she was supposed to do. I took care of my sister."

KILLING DAD

Stacey was also rumored to have been behind the murder of her father, Jerry Daniels, in February of 2002.

Michael's brother in law, John Corbett, found out that Daniels was hospitalized for a lung ailment. His condition was improving until his daughter Stacey visited.

Daniels would day soon after her visit and Corbett recalled Stacey giving him a can of soda for him to drink.

Stacey then had her father cremated and took control over his estate.

NEW HUSBAND

Stacey would start dating again, settling on David Castor. David was the polar opposite of Michael. He didn't party, didn't drink and had his own business. He had a stability that Stacey always wanted.

"He had money," Ashley said. "And my Mom was happy with that."

"He was attracted to Stacey because she accepted him," David Castor Jr said. "I think he just wanted someone there with him."

The new couple looked like peas in a pod. David had red hair just like Janice. He also had a thick, out of style mustache just like Michael Wallace before him. He looked like a scaled down version of Chicago Bear football coach Mike Ditka and had the fiery personality to match.

David had been married before to Janice Poissant. The two had a child together, David Jr, and had a happy marriage until David suffered a head injury during a motorcycle accident. He experienced amnesia for a long period of time and eventually got his memory back. His personality changed, however, and he would be a lot more brusque in his demeanor. He would soon prefer material goods over people. He would verbally abuse Janice until she finally decided to leave him after twenty-six years of marriage.

David had his own air conditioning installation and repair company which he purchased from Janice's father. His father-in-law had taught him everything about the business from the ground up. Janice and mother-in-law would work in the office while he went out on service calls. After his marriage to Janice ended, David's business began to flounder. His father-in-law bailed him out, however, and helped him put the business back on its feet.

Stacey would eventually replace Janice not only in marriage but in the business as well, becoming his office manager.

David didn't have Michael's substance abuse problems but he loved his toys. He would purchase motorcycles, jet skis, snowmobiles, and boats. His spending habits would cause a rift with his wife.

"They did fight because my Mom paid the majority of the bills," Ashley said. "And David just paid for his toys."

The marriage of blended families would cause a rift between the children. The girls did not take kindly to David's personality. He thought his controlling ways would keep the girls in line. Instead, his rules and regulations had the opposite effect.

The girls would rebel.

"At first, we didn't get along at all," Ashley said.

David had issues with the girls. He didn't allow his first wife an allowance and made it clear to the girls that he was the man "large and in charge."

Ashley would stand up to him first. She was older than Bree and had the bigger mouth. Stacey would intervene and do her best to try and make the girls see the positive benefit of living with David. They were closer to their school and had a bigger house.

The girls, however, had gotten used to being a threesome.

"David made it very clear that he didn't want any more kids," Bree recalled. "He didn't want to be our father and he didn't want to act like it."

He would send the teenage girls mixed signals, on one hand giving them the cold shoulder but on occasion trying to be their friend.

David and Ashley did eventually mend their ways as when she graduated from school she saw the 'proud father' look on his face.

"He wasn't trying to be like a Dad," Ashley recalled. "But like a friend."

"It is hard to tell what was going through David's mind when he married Stacey," Orange said. "He was probably one of those men who just couldn't stand to be alone. He would hold his step-daughters at arm's length but deep down it appears that he wanted their affection. He just didn't know how to reciprocate it."

MORE MARRIAGE TROUBLE

While David appeared to be building bridges with the girls, the gap between he and his wife was widening. They would fight on a regular basis until they had a huge argument on their anniversary weekend. David wanted to go away while Stacey had other plans.

She would claim they fought throughout the day and that David went to his bedroom and locked himself in. She then sent both of her daughters to go stay with friends while she went off by herself to leave David alone.

David didn't arrive at his workplace the next day and Stacey "thought something was wrong." She called the sheriff's department and told them that he had locked himself in the bedroom. He wasn't responding to her knocks at the door nor was he responding to her texts. She told authorities that he was "depressed" and "maybe suicidal."

Sheriffs arrived and kicked in the door of the bedroom only to find David lying dead in a pool of vomit.

Near his body was a container of anti-freeze and a half-empty glass of the green liquid.

"He's not dead," Stacey screamed as she saw his prone body. "He's not dead!"

Detectives would confiscate the evidence from the scene although it had the obvious look of a suicide.

With her husband declared dead, Stacey called her daughters on the phone.

"I have something bad to tell you," the crying mother said. "And I don't know how to tell you. 'Well, what?' David killed himself."

The coroner would state that David killed himself by drinking a lethal amount of the anti-freeze. But an alert investigator noticed a turkey baster in the garbage can outside the garage. He took the item as evidence and had it tested.

"Something didn't feel right to the investigators," Orange said. "Luckily one of them had a sixth sense about the situation. Something about Stacey seemed a bit off as did the so-called suicide itself. Men typically do not take the passive way out of drinking poison or sleeping pills. They most commonly commit suicide by blowing their brains out. David owned a shotgun. That remained untouched. Yet he chose to commit suicide by ingesting anti-freeze which would be a really painful way to go. Why suffer when you can have it over and done with a pull of the trigger."

The forensic analysis would reveal Stacey's fingerprints as the only ones on the glass on David's bedside table. They also discovered that the turkey baster at David's DNA at the tip.

"If the door was locked," Orange said. "Then how did the turkey baster end up in the garage with his DNA."

This evidence led them to believe that Stacey had "force fed" the anti-freeze to David who was too weak to fight back.

"She had drugged him asleep," Orange said. "If you near death or unconscious you are not going to notice someone dripping anti-freeze into your mouth."

Investigators began making inquiries among David's friends and family. They kept getting the same answer.

"David wouldn't commit suicide."

Authorities didn't play their hand just yet. They played dumb, allowing Stacey to believe she was in the clear. They wiretapped her house and listened in on her calls for any incriminating statements. They then set up cameras that monitored both her house and the graves of her husbands as Stacey had them buried side by side.

"You had Mike on the far left," Corbett said. "David on the far right. I said 'what's she doing, starting a collection up there?'"

"She had her name engraved on both of the headstones," Bree said. "It's kinda weird."

But Stacey would never visit the graveyard where her husbands were buried. She did call a friend but told the friend that she "didn't do any of it."

Investigators needed more proof and decided to have Michael's body exhumed. They ran tests on his body that would reveal that he had ingested the anti-freeze just like David.

Back at home, Stacey was oblivious to the investigation. She went about her days in a daze, ignoring her daughters.

"After David died," Ashley recalled. "It was just as before. She didn't want to do things with me and my sister."

COLLECTING CASH

Stacey would benefit from receiving David's estate. His own son felt shock and hurt when he find out he was left out of the will.

"Things had deteriorated between us after the divorce," David Jr said. "And it hurt."

It would later be revealed that Stacey had doctored David's will to exclude his son and give all proceeds of his estate to her. She had a friend who was a notary who later admitted to helping Stacey with forging the document.

Stacey would inherit the home and the air conditioning business which she quickly sold for a profit.

"There was so much sweat that went into that business," David Jr said. "My grandfather started that business. And she just threw it away."

Stacey would receive $200,000 free and clear.

KILLING ASHLEY

By September 2007, Stacey felt the noose tightening around her neck. She eventually found out about the police exhuming Michael's body and finding the lethal dose of anti-freeze that she administered. Then the sheriff's arrived at her door.

One of the sheriffs described Stacey as having the 'deer in the headlights' look as they approached. The normally cool and collected Stacey stammered during their interrogation and mistakenly referred to a news story wherein the wife had poisoned her husband using "anti-free".

One of the sheriffs noted that she used the word 'anti-free' as opposed to 'anti-freeze'. This would later prove to be a huge mistake on Stacey's part.

Stacey would return home and she desperately needed a way out. She needed someone to take the blame. A blood sacrifice.

Even it was her own daughter.

Police would arrive on Ashley's college campus (Bryant & Stratton) to question her about her father's death. It was Ashley's first day of school and they informed her that stepfather had been poisoned instead of having a heart attack.

Ashley became angry at the investigators. She was insulted that they would even think that her mother could kill her father.

"I didn't believe that she did it," Ashley said. "I never thought for a second that she would ever hurt anybody. They couldn't figure out why he killed himself. They were just trying to pin it on somebody else."

Ashley was in disbelief and called her mother. Stacey invited her home.

"You've been through enough," Stacey said. "Come home and let's get drunk."

Ashley agreed, still trusting her mother as her 'best friend.' She arrived home and Stacey gave her a 'nasty-tasting' drink. It was a mixture of Vodka and Sprite.

And unknown to Ashley, anti-freeze was added to the cocktail.

"Just keep stirring it," Stacey told her daughter who spat up the drink. "It has Sprite in it."

"All I remember was going to sleep at one o'clock on Thursday," Ashley recalled. "Then when I wake up it isn't Thursday anymore it's Friday."

Hours later, Ashley would be found in a coma-like state by her sister Bree. She screamed for her mother to call 911 before seeing a note beside Ashley.

"I found this note by Ashley's bed," Bree recalled. "And it said all of this stuff, 'Dear Mommy, I'm sorry. And it was typed. And I was like 'Oh my God, you have to see this.'"

Stacey knew exactly what was happening to her daughter. Yet she played the role of the distraught mother to the hilt.

"My daughter has taken some pills," Stacey choked back tears as she spoke to the dispatcher. "It sounds like there's something in her throat. Ashley. Oh my God. Oh my God. Oh my God."

Medics would rush to home and take Ashley to the hospital. They had discovered she had ingested a lethal dose of painkillers. Stacey had crushed pain medication pills and poured them in Ashley's drink, creating a lethal cocktail. Had the paramedics arrived only minutes later, Ashley would have been dead.

Stacey made sure that the "confession" letter made it to the hands of the paramedics. The typewritten letter was over a page long, single-spaced, with Ashley giving details and specifics as to why she killed both her father and stepfather. At the end of the confession, she pleads for her mother "to forgive her."

Stacey did not expect her daughter to make it through. To her surprise, her daughter was revived and quickly questioned by police.

"It was all blurry," Ashley said. "All I remember was a man in a red shirt yelling, 'What did you drink? What did you take? What did you write in that note?'"

"The last thing I remember was my Mom giving me a drink," Ashley said. "It was something she had never done before."

The police officer was adamant about asking Ashley if she wrote the suicide note.

"I didn't write any notes," Ashley said, appearing confused about the question.

Witnessing the entire exchange, Bree would be the one to break the news to Ashley.

Their mother had tried to kill her.

ARRESTED AT LAST

Authorities would spend over two years accumulating evidence against Stacey. In 2007, she would be arrested for degree murder in David's death and for attempting to murder Ashley as well as frame her for the killings of David and Michael.

Ashley would be brought to the stand and testify that she did not kill David or Michael. She also said that she did not type up the computer-generated "confession" letter where she revealed that she killed both men. Stacey made a mistake in that she had prepared numerous drafts of Ashley's "confession" later on her computer. The drafts had timestamps and had been written while Ashley was away at college, proving that she could not have written the letters.

There was also repeated use of the word "anti-free" throughout the letter. This phrasing echoed what she had said during her interrogation with police.

Mounting further evidence, prosecuting attorneys argued that David's "suicide" didn't make any sense because his fingerprints were not on the glass of anti-freeze they found by his side. They stated that he had been force-fed the poison through the turkey baster. Stacey argued otherwise, saying that David got the idea after watching a documentary on Lynn Turner, a woman who would murder her lovers by using the poison.

"He was depressed lot," Stacey said. "The business wasn't going well."

THE DEFENSE

Stacey's defense team began attacking Ashley. They wanted to prove that she was someone capable of murder, even at age eleven.

They began documenting how Michael showed favoritism to Bree and that Ashley killed him out of jealousy. Belaboring the point, they said that Ashley never got along with her stepfather David and killed him out of jealousy as well.

Stacey would then be called to the stand. She stated that she thought Ashley was mentally ill. The prosecuting team then went to work on Stacey, shouting out their questions in an accusatory manner. They asked why if Ashley was mentally ill she had not one shred of medical history to corroborate that allegation.

Then came the coup de grace. The prosecution team revealed to the jury that it was Stacey's fingerprints alone on the "confession" letter and not Ashley's. They had wiretapped the home and stated that there were 'typing sounds' throughout the day.

The sounds of Stacey typing up the fake 'confession' letter.

The jury deliberated for only two days before pronouncing Stacey guilty on February 5th, 2009 of second-degree murder in the death of David and attempted murder for overdosing Ashley with drugs and Vodka

The judge ordered her to serve a maximum of 25 years to life for the murder of David and another 25 for the attempt to kill Ashley. An additional 1 to 4 years was added for forging David's will.

Ashley still retained mixed feelings about her mother as it all came as a shock to her.

"I never knew what hate was until now," Ashley said. "Even though I do hate her, I still love her at the same time. That bothers me, it is so confusing. How can you hate someone and love them at the same time? I just wish that she would say sorry for everything she did, including all the lies. As horrible as it makes me feel, this is goodbye mom. As hard as you tried, I survived and I will survive because now I'm surrounded by people that love me. I'm going to do good things in this world despite making me in every sense of the word an orphan."

RANTINGS OF A SOCIOPATH

Stacey would be admitted into the Bedford Hills Correctional Facility for Women in Bedford Hills, New York.

Stacey would continue to place guilt on her daughter, Ashley. "She brought this on," Stacey said. "Bree was an innocent victim in all of this. I lost her, I lost my husbands."

"I was happy that they said she was guilty," Bree said. "Because we all know that she's guilty."

Ashley would be haunted by her mother's betrayal forever.

"I would have done anything for her," Ashley said. "But she tried to kill me instead."

DEATH

Stacey would be found dead in her cell on June 11th, 2016. Her cause of death remains under investigation.

FATAL ATTRACTION : THE TRUE STORY OF CAROLYN WARMUS

SUSAN BUTLER

Carolyn Warmus is serving a sentence of 25 years to life in Bedford Hills Correctional Facility for Women for murdering the wife of her lover, a fellow elementary school teacher.

Her case was widely referred to in the media as the "Fatal Attraction murder" in reference to the 1987 movie.

She was 25 years old at the time of the murder in 1989, and 28 when she was convicted in 1992 after two trials.

Neighbors and acquaintances, from her time in Michigan and from her time in New York, described her as pleasant and sunny. One was quoted as saying she was the kind of girl you could take home to Mom.

People who knew her better said that her big grin hid an emotionally disturbed, needy, often depressed, and occasionally suicidal individual.

In her 20's, blond, wide-eyed Carolyn had a sexy personality, a great figure, and dressed expensively and fashionably. She turned heads. Her employers described her as cheerful and very competent.

In her 20's, she had also begun obsessing over a string of older unavailable men and, by the time of the murder, had a long history of bizarre behavior—some of it criminal—in relation to these romantic entanglements.

Early life

Carolyn Warmus was born on January 8, 1964. She was the eldest of three children of millionaire Thomas Warmus and his wife

Elizabeth. The family lived in small affluent neighborhoods around Troy, Michigan, a suburb of Detroit.

In 1958, Thomas Warmus had begun a career as a life insurance agent. In 1963, he formed the American Way Service Corporation, which later became a holding company for a number of insurance companies. He was a millionaire by the time he was raising his family.

Carolyn and her younger sister and brother—Tracey and Tommy—had a typical wealthy upbringing and lifestyle. They were not lacking in material comforts.

However, a family acquaintance told People Magazine in 1990 that there was no deep emotional bond between the parents and their children. A childhood friend told People that none of the children had a good relationship with their father, who was obsessed with business and a rich lifestyle. Their mother was also more interested in being a socialite than in being a mother.

Elizabeth Warmus filed for divorce in 1970. The Warmus' marriage had been difficult for years. When they divorced in 1972, Carolyn was eight years old. By this time, American Way Service Corp. was worth $107 million.

Thomas Warmus married his secretary, Nancy, who was younger and wore mink coats, tight strapless sequined dresses, and liked expensive sports cars.

Elizabeth won custody of the children and they lived with her in Birmingham, Michigan, another Detroit suburb. Thomas built Nancy a huge fenced-in house on a hill in the new-money neighborhood of Franklin Village.

When Carolyn was 14, Elizabeth remarried and moved to the East Coast. The children did not go with her. They moved to the big house in Franklin Village. Carolyn told a friend that the house was always empty. She and Tracey used it to throw lavish parties.

High school

Carolyn attended Seaholm High School and graduated in 1981 with honors. She was athletic, cheerful, blond and attractive, got good grades, and played on the basketball team.

Peers who knew her well said that her sunny façade hid deep emotional problems caused by the bitter divorce of her parents and lack of affection from her parents, especially her father.

She and her sister were rivals. Tracey was more popular and better looking, which Carolyn found upsetting.

Schoolmates who were interviewed for a February 1990 People Magazine article painted a disturbing picture of the teenaged Carolyn. They said she tried to buy popularity and affection by inviting people to her family's Florida home, throwing extravagant parties, and throwing cash around. In her senior year, she paid a classmate $100 to set her up with a guy she had her eye on.

The $100 date told People his involvement with Carolyn lasted a few months, and he was happy to get her out of his life when it ended. He described her as an extremely unhappy person who complained about having no father and no affection. He said she sometimes talked about suicide.

University of Michigan

After high school, Carolyn attended the University of Michigan and graduated in 1985 with a Bachelor of Science (Psychology). She was already a very troubled person by the time she went to college and became increasingly so. Friends who knew her in college said that suffered from depression and occasionally spoke of suicide.

Some of her acquaintances told police later that she was "ditzy" and "schizo."

While attending university, Carolyn had a series of relationships with older men who were attached that ended badly and left her feeling like a victim. She was apparently incapable of maintaining a successful relationship, and she behaved obsessively during and after her entanglements.

It has been theorized that her attraction to these unattainable men, and her going to extremes to get them back after they broke up with her—or to get back at them—stemmed from her poor relationship with her father. She was, after all, desirable enough to interest any attainable man she wanted.

Paul Laven

In February 1983, while attending the University of Michigan, Carolyn met a teaching assistant named Paul Laven. By June, they were dating.

According to people who knew them, he was never serious about her, but she was obsessed with him. In everything she did, she had him in mind. If someone paid her a compliment about an outfit or a hairdo, she would ask them what Paul would think of it.

Paul Laven broke up with Carolyn in December and soon announced his engagement to another student, Wendy Siegel.

Carolyn began stalking and harassing the couple. Records from a court complaint filed by Paul show that Carolyn's behavior became obsessive and disturbing. The way she later described the situation to private investigator Jim Russo was that she had tried and tried to win him back after he married someone else and it hadn't worked.

She followed Paul around campus, harassed him at his office, and phoned him day and night.

The couple moved to another town and got an unlisted phone number.

On April 6, Carolyn conned a phone company employee into giving her that unlisted number. On April 10, she entered Paul and Wendy's apartment and had to be removed by police. She had also been harassing Paul at his office.

In May 1984, she left a note on Paul's car claiming that she was pregnant with his baby and begging him to phone her.

After returning from a vacation in Florida, Carolyn left Wendy a deliberately misspelled note that said she hoped Wendy had enjoyed the past week of Carolyn not bothering her because now she could start worrying again since Carolyn was back.

She added that Wendy would have even more to compete with now, because of Carolyn's tan. That gives some insight into Carolyn's mind: she thought a tan was relevant.

She went on to say that, of course, "with a body like mine" Wendy had to realize what tough competition she was up against, that Wendy was now just about out of the running completely, and that Paul would probably continue to pretend to care about Wendy as long as she let him live with her.

Laven and Siegel were granted a temporary restraining order against Warmus two weeks before their July 1984 wedding to prevent her from wrecking their wedding or reception.

After their wedding, they obtained a permanent order restraining Warmus from communicating with them "forever" and from interfering with their "rights of privacy" and their "rights to travel."

Carolyn's family was Catholic, but she had begun taking instruction to convert to Judaism while she was dating Paul Laven, who was Jewish. She converted to Judaism in her final semester, which was almost a year after Laven and Siegel were married.

Her instructor, Rabbi David Nelson of the Congregation Beth Shalom, Oak Park, described Carolyn as intelligent and quiet.

He assumed she was taking instruction in order to marry a Jewish husband, but noted that she was never accompanied to her classes by anyone. This was unusual. She attended her conversion ceremony alone as well, which he said was very unusual.

Carolyn chose the Hebrew name Chana Ariela, "gracious lioness of god."

Summer after graduating from University of Michigan

After Carolyn graduated from the University of Michigan, she moved back to the home of her father and stepmother in Franklin Village and spent the summer of 1985 preparing to move to New York.

She found a summer job as a waitress at a nightclub in Royal Oak, Michigan, called the Juke Box. It was a rock and roll bar where booze was cheap and the pretty waitresses danced on the bar for the patrons.

In the opinion of Peter Sherman, bouncer, Carolyn fit right in. She had a great smile, a great figure, and a great attitude. She was never in a bad mood, he said.

Credit Cards

The bar manager, Debbie Mullin, said that Carolyn was pulling off credit card fraud while she worked at the Juke Box. She was ultimately fired for it. Federal investigators investigated, but Warmus was never prosecuted because the investigators couldn't find enough evidence to make the charges stick.

According to Mullin, Carolyn used a classic trick: she would run a card through the credit card imprinting machine two or three times, use one imprint for the real credit card customer, and use the others for customers who paid cash. She would then keep the cash instead of putting it in the cash register.

Brian "Buddy" Fetter

Carolyn met a businessman named Brian Fetter, nicknamed Buddy, while working at the Juke Box. They had dated. Bouncer Peter Sherman said that Fetter showed up one day to ask what the heck was going on with Carolyn.

According to Sherman, Fetter told him that she had been hounding him. She had been leaving him so many phone messages that he had been forced to change his number. That was when Sherman first realized there was something truly off about Carolyn.

NYC, Master's Degree, Parco and Russo and the married bartender

Carolyn moved to New York City in 1985 after leaving the Juke Box. She earned a Master's degree in elementary education in 1987 at Teacher's College, Columbia University. In New York, her pattern of relationships with inappropriate men and stalking continued.

She was living in Manhattan when she had an affair with a married bartender who lived and worked in New Jersey.

One afternoon in the summer of 1987, Carolyn waltzed into the office of Vincent Parco, the private investigator who later testified about having sold Warmus a gun. She had apparently found him in the yellow pages.

Parco was a man who lived large and loved to be around young women. Carolyn looked prim but hot in a white tennis outfit. Parco's investigative specialty was sniffing out illegal tenants, but Warmus wanted to put her married bartender under surveillance.

Parco assigned Jim Russo to the case. Carolyn wanted to go along on the mission. This was not standard operating procedure, but Russo brought her along.

They drove to the bartender's house and then to the Ramada where he worked. The bar was not busy enough for Russo to take pictures without being noticed. Back in the car with Warmus, Russo found her pleasant, vivacious, and talkative. She asked him if he was married and if his wife minded his long hours.

She talked about herself. She talked about a man she had been seeing in Michigan who had married somebody else. She talked about how she had tried so hard to get that man back but nothing worked. She talked about the new boyfriend—the bartender—and how everything was finally okay because of him.

Then the reason for the surveillance came out. The bartender had promised to leave his wife for Carolyn and he was too slow about it. Carolyn wanted to send the bartender's wife some compromising photos that would move the situation along. (Possibly, the bartender had never made any such promise, in good faith or bad, but had simply tired of her.)

Russo was not able to catch the bartender doing anything incriminating. The surveillance was a bust. According to Russo, Parco and Warmus then cooked up a scheme to solve that problem. They could superimpose photos of Carolyn in sexy poses on photos of the bartender.

Russo claimed he would not have gone along with faking evidence, but he was willing to take riské pictures of Warmus. She posed in a variety of sexual poses in see-through outfits and skimpy lingerie while Russo took photos.

He delivered the film to Parco.

According to Russo, a few days later he saw evidence on Parco's desk that Parco and Warmus were trying to put together a cut-and-paste with the photos of Carolyn and photos that someone else had taken of the bartender.

That plan also seems to have been a bust. It might have worked out if Photoshop had existed back then. Maybe Carolyn had already lost interest in the bartender and his wife and abandoned the plan.

After that, Russo saw Warmus around Parco's office a couple of times a week for a while. He suspected that the relationship between Warmus and Parco became intimate at some point.

Forgery

In Carolyn's murder trials, the issue of forged telephone records came up. The prosecution tried to introduce a previous instance of Carolyn committing forgery.

In June 1987, a woman was involved in car accident and identified herself to the other driver as Carolyn Warmus. Later, to establish an alibi against the subsequent damage claim, Carolyn wrote to the other driver stating that on the day of the collision she had been a chaperone on a school trip out of state.

She included a letter signed by school official Dr. Richard Sprague to back up her claim. The lawyer for the other side of the damage claim dropped the case.

Later, while following Warmus' trial, that lawyer sent a copy of the letter to Dr. Sprague. Sprague said he had not written the letter, the signature was not his, that particular school trip did not occur on that date, and Carolyn was not on that trip when it did occur.

She certainly could not have been on a school trip in June 1987, since she wasn't hired by the Westchester County school system until September.

Carolyn's trial judge refused to allow the letter into evidence on grounds that it would be too prejudicial.

Westchester County School System

In September 1987, after getting her Master's Degree, Carolyn was hired by the public elementary school system of Westchester County, New York. She served as a substitute for teachers on maternity leave. She also began work on her Doctorate of Education at Columbia.

After her time working as a substitute, she was hired without reservation by the Byram Hills school district to work at Coman Hill Elementary School.

The personnel director of Byram Hills, Dr. Linda Ochser, told The New York Times that she was impressed by Carolyn's academic credentials and that Carolyn had sailed through their interview process as an outstanding candidate. Dr. Ochser described Warmus as a "very vivacious, upbeat teacher."

But some of Carolyn's co-workers later told police that she was a nut and had several personalities.

Greenville School and meeting Paul Solomon

Carolyn's first substitute teaching job was at Greenville Elementary in Scarsdale, New York. Here the 23-year-old met yet another married man, 38-year-old Paul Solomon, also an elementary school teacher. As the more experienced teacher, he has been described as having been her mentor. He has been described as being gentle, understanding, and mentoring towards younger female teachers in general.

It is not known exactly when their relationship became sexual. Paul's wife, Betty Jeanne, did not mention any suspicions to anybody.

Paul testified later that he cared for Carolyn, felt guilty about the sex, wanted to break up with her, wasn't going to divorce his wife, and that he and Warmus had intercourse and oral sex several times throughout the year. "It's very hard to resist Carolyn," he said.

He was drawn to her youth, good looks, taut body, outgoing and fun personality—though he also found her possessive and unpredictable.

Carolyn had a duplex apartment above the Catch A Rising Star comedy club in Manhattan and soon they were meeting there. They also met in hotel rooms and had sex in Carolyn's car.

In December, Carolyn received a card from Paul that said he was falling in love with her.

Another note from Paul said, "If you're smart you'll do one of two things. Turn away and never see me again and save yourself from the pain and hurt, or keep loving me and take the risk of you and I having something together forever."

Around this time, Carolyn told a University of Michigan friend on the phone that she was dating a married man who was going to leave his wife for her.

Warmus' next substitute posting, partly through that school year, was at Pleasantville School. Her relationship with Solomon continued.

Paul and Betty Jeanne

Betty Jeanne's high school sweetheart, Earl, who she had been planning to marry, was killed in a car crash during her freshman year in college. In the spring of 1967, she met Paul Solomon.

College friends describe Betty Jeanne as a happy, agreeable, helpful girl and Paul as intense, competitive, confrontational, and someone who wanted to be important. They say she became quiet and reclusive under his influence.

A former roommate of Betty Jeanne's told New York Magazine that he was domineering, possessive, and jealous, that he told her what to wear, what sorority to join, and what friends to drop.

Another friend told New York Magazine that Betty Jeanne was sweet and Paul was not nice, and added that Paul was rude to Betty Jeanne. Friends were surprised when they married. But Betty Jeanne was in love with Paul.

Their wedding was in 1970. Betty Jeanne had dropped out of school a couple of years earlier. Paul had just left school and joined the Air Force.

Their daughter, Kristan, was born in 1973. Shortly after that, Paul left the Air Force to go back to school and finish his degree. Then he was hired as a teacher at Greenville Elementary School, which was in one of the richest school districts in the country.

Betty Jeanne worked as a bank teller and made her way up the ranks to branch manager. In 1984, she left the bank for a better paying job with a collection agency. They bought their Greenburgh condominium in 1987.

At the time of her 1989 murder, Betty Jeanne was 40 years old and an account executive with Continental Credit Corporation.

The Solomons were comfortable, but they were middle class. Most of Kristan's friends had wealthy parents. The Solomons could not give their daughter all the things her friends had.

To increase their income, Paul started coaching sports throughout the school year and in the summer. He also took up basketball, bowling, and golf to keep fit. Those activities kept him away from home most evenings. Betty Jeanne developed her own interests in addition to her job and got involved in civic activities.

Both of the Solomons were always busy. Their condo was a home for the daughter they both adored, but it also became just a place to grab a meal and go off again.

Paul was a good teacher. Some of his earlier prickliness had softened and he had morphed into a good authority figure for students needing a firm hand.

He insisted on being the authority figure at home as well, though, and Betty Jeanne told her mother she was sick of this. Paul was also still subjecting Betty Jeanne to the occasional rudeness that had made her college friends uncomfortable.

Betty Jeanne considered leaving Paul several times, but she never did. According to testimony in Carolyn's trials, both Paul and Betty Jeanne were having affairs but they were not ready to put an end to their marriage.

Paul and Carolyn and Paul's family

Paul introduced Carolyn to Kristan one evening while he was coaching Kristan's basketball team. Carolyn tried to play a role as a friend of the family or a big sister to Kristan. She gave Kristan expensive gifts and took her shopping. One night, Kristan went to a show in Manhattan with Paul, Carolyn, and another teacher.

In early 1988, all three Solomons were out to dinner with Carolyn when Carolyn offered to take Kristan on a ski trip during the upcoming school break. (Carolyn's University of Michigan freshman yearbook lists her interests as skiing and travel).

Betty Jeanne told her sister Joyce about the planned trip and said that people were teasing her about letting her daughter go on this trip with a bimbo. Joyce wanted to know if Carolyn was afraid they would go bar hopping. But Carolyn told her sister that Carolyn seemed like a nice enough woman, and she didn't want to spoil her daughter's fun.

On that ski trip, Carolyn told Kristan that she was concerned that Betty Jeanne didn't like her very much. Kristan knew that Carolyn was right but kindly tried to persuade her otherwise.

Summer 1988

In the summer of 1988, Paul temporarily broke off his affair with Carolyn.

According to trial testimony, during that summer Carolyn told a Michigan friend Ryan Attenson that "with her money," she and Paul and "Paul's family" would have "a perfect life together." She was going to make sure that she ended up with him. She also told Attenson that she was thinking of hiring a private investigator to prove to Paul that Betty Jeanne was cheating on him.

During that summer of 1988, Carolyn wrote notes to Paul and gave Kristan extravagant presents. For Kristan's birthday in August, Warmus dropped by unexpectedly with a bracelet and two outfits. Kristan later testified that she was hesitant about this visit, because she knew her mom didn't enjoy having Warmus in the house, and she was afraid they would "have words."

Carolyn visited Jim Russo's new office a few times during the summer and fall of 1988. (In February, Russo had left Vincent Parco to form his own investigation firm.)

On one visit, she claimed that one of her father's airplanes had exploded or crashed on a runway and that it was sabotage. On another visit, she said that her sister had been the victim of a hit-and-run driver. Carolyn mentioned a short dark-haired woman in relations to both of these incidents.

Again in Russo's office, a few months before the murder, Warmus told Russo that she had seen this woman before and that the woman's name was "Jean or Betty Jean." Russo testified that Carolyn begged for protection against this woman who was threatening her family. He suggested a bodyguard, but she asked for a gun and a silencer.

According to trial witness Lisa Kattai, Lisa and Carolyn had worked together at a temp job in August 1988 and were friendly. Kattai's driver's license went missing on that job. Carolyn had access to Kattai's purse at the time.

According to her testimony, Kattai's hairstyle in that license photo looked much the same as Warmus' hairstyle at the time the license disappeared. Kattai reported the loss when it happened, and she thought no more of it. She had no opinion as to whether or not Warmus had anything to do with the disappearance of the license.

Later, the prosecution would suggest that Warmus used Kattai's driver's license for I.D. when she bought gun ammunition.

Fall 1988 and early 1989

Paul Solomon and Carolyn Warmus resumed their sexual relationship in the fall of 1988 even though, according to his testimony, he had conflicting feelings and felt guilty.

Vincent Parco testified at trial that Carolyn had hounded him for months before the murder to get her a gun for protection against burglars that were running rampant in her neighborhood. She finally broke through his resistance in the first week of January 1989 and he sold her an unregistered .25 caliber Beretta pistol with bullets and a homemade silencer for $2,500.

Patricia January, a school nurse, testified that a week before the murder Carolyn told her that she owned a gun because living alone was terrifying.

The murder

On January 15, 1989, a Sunday, Kristan was away on a ski trip with friends. Betty Jeanne and Paul were watching TV. Carolyn phoned at 1:37 p.m.

Carolyn wanted to know why Paul hadn't taken her out for her 25th birthday on January 8. They agreed to meet at 7:30 p.m. at Treetops, a restaurant in the Holiday Inn at Yonkers. Paul told Betty Jeanne he was going bowling that night. They had a confrontation about it.

He hooked his car up to a battery charger sometime that afternoon. Since his wife would be staying home that night, he could use her car that evening. (Later, one of the prosecutors, pushing a conspiracy theory, hinted that the battery charger cable was meant to be an arrow to the murder site for a hitman.)

Paul left home around 6:30 p.m., made an appearance at the bowling alley, and left the bowling alley at 7:15 p.m. He drove to Treetops in Betty Jeanne's car and waited for Carolyn.

Shortly before 7:12 p.m., New York Telephone Company operator Linda Viana Newcombe answered a 911 call from a woman in distress. Newcombe was not able to say at trial if the caller had said "he is trying to kill me" or "she is trying to kill me." But she was sure she heard "trying to kill me" before the call went dead.

Newcombe immediately reported the call to police. Sources differ as to whether the operator got the number wrong and therefore reported it to the wrong police detachment, or she got the number right but the reverse directory was not up to date. Either way, the police went to the wrong home, they did not find Betty Jeanne on the living room floor, and they did not save her.

At about 7:45 p.m., Carolyn walked into the Treetops bar to meet up with Paul. They had drinks and a meal. The waitress saw them deep in conversation. They were there for almost two hours.

Paul later told the jury that he told Carolyn she should seek her future elsewhere. He said, "I'd be so happy to dance at your wedding and see you happy." Her answer to that was, "What about your happiness, Paul? Don't you deserve to be happy?" His answer to that was, "If anything happens to Betty Jeanne and me, I'd never get married anyway."

After this effort at pushing her away, he went to the parking lot and sat in Carolyn's car. He allowed her to give him oral sex. In a few minutes, they were finished. They promised to meet again soon and went their separate ways.

At 11:42 p.m., Paul arrived home at his Greenburgh condo and found Betty Jeanne's body on the living room floor. He called the Village of Scarsdale Police Department. "It's my wife! I think she's dead! I need help. My name is Paul Solomon. She's not moving. She's covered with blood! Please hurry!"

Scarsdale Police notified Greenburgh Police who dispatched units to the scene. They found a distraught Paul Solomon and Betty Jeanne lying in a pool of blood.

It was later determined that Betty Jeanne had received nine bullets in her back and legs and had been pistol-whipped about her head.

Nobody had heard the gunshots. The only sign of a struggle was a disconnected phone jack. There was no sign of forced entry. Police photographs of the scene showed a black wool glove near the body. This glove later nailed Carolyn.

Investigation January 1989 - Paul

Paul Solomon was the initial suspect. He admitted to police that he'd had an affair with Carolyn for the past year, that they'd had a date at Treetops after he went to the bowling alley on the night of the murder, and even that they'd had sex in Carolyn's car in the parking lot after the date.

Police had been able to substantiate his alibi of going bowling and then hooking up with Carolyn. The investigators started looking for another suspect.

Very soon, Solomon broke off his relationship with Carolyn again and took up with a new girlfriend, Barbara Ballor.

Investigation January 1989 - Carolyn

Carolyn, on the advice of her father's lawyer Mr. Fiore, took a polygraph test on January 20 as a precautionary measure. It recorded truthful responses when she was asked if she had murdered Betty Jeanne and if she had been in the apartment when Betty Jeanne was murdered.

It was a bit iffy about whether or not she was protecting anyone. Polygraph results are not admissible in court.

Investigation March/April 1989 - Carolyn and phone records and guns

Once Paul had been ruled out, police looked into other options: professional hit, a burglary gone bad, aborted sex crime. By March 1989, none of those had panned out. Eventually, they turned their attention again to Warmus.

Detective Richard Constantino spent two months investigating Carolyn's phone records from immediately before and after the murder. The records revealed that many conversations had taken place between Vincent Parco and Carolyn Warmus immediately before and after the murder.

Parco gave police a series of different reasons for those phone conversations. His stories kept changing. Eventually, he relented and admitted that Carolyn had wanted a gun with a silencer and he had provided them.

Parco's friend George Peters had made the silencer. Peters had test fired the gun into a block of wood in the process of making the silencer, and police matched a casing from his workshop to a casing found next to Betty Jeanne's body.

In addition to all the calls between Warmus and Parco, investigators found a call from Carolyn to a gun store at 3:02 p.m. on the day of Betty Jeanne's murder. Carolyn and Paul had just spoken on the phone at 1:37 p.m. that day and set up their date for later that evening, and Carolyn knew that Kristan out of town skiing.

The gun store was called Ray's Sport Shop and it was in North Plainfield, New Jersey, twenty miles west of Manhattan. Investigators drove to the shop and found that only one person from outside of New Jersey, and only one female—those being the same person—had bought .25 caliber ammunition there that day. That person had used a driver's license in the name of Lisa Kattai for I.D.

Police visited Lisa and she told them about her disappeared driver's license from the previous summer. They soon ascertained that Lisa had not been the purchaser of the ammunition and that she had worked in an office with Carolyn.

June 1989 – stalking again

Carolyn Warmus had begun pursuing Paul Solomon again, soon after the murder. In June 1989, she followed Paul to Puerto Rico.

She didn't realize that Paul was taking the trip with a new girlfriend, Barbara Ballow, in tow.

Doing anything to interject herself into the situation, Carolyn called Ballor's family on the phone. She pretended to be a police officer and began making wild accusations about Ballor in an effort to get them to break up the relationship.

After returning from Puerto Rico, Ballor obtained a protection order against Carolyn Warmus.

August 1989 – hospitalized

On August 8, 1989, Carolyn's neighbors reported bizarre behavior at her Upper East Side Manhattan address, 1485 First Avenue. Officers arrived and found Carolyn to be emotionally disturbed and at risk of harming herself. She was subsequently sent to the psych ward for a week.

Arrest and first indictments (dismissed)

Carolyn Warmus was indicted for second-degree murder and weapons possession on February 2, 1990. On February 6, she was freed on $250,000 bail, the bond having been posted by her father.

On April 4, 1990, Associated Press reported that Warmus' lawyer, David Lewis, had asked for the indictments to be dismissed due to prosecutorial misconduct in the form of grand jury leaks to the press.

On August 7, 1990, The Day, a Connecticut newspaper, reported that Judge John Carey had dismissed the indictments on grounds that the "integrity of the grand jury proceeding was impaired." The reasons given by the judge were that the state had concealed an immunity agreement with a key prosecution witness and that instructions to the grand jury were faulty.

Vincent Parco, who had sold the pistol to Carolyn, had been granted immunity in exchange for his testimony.

First trial

The prosecution obtained a new indictment for second-degree murder against Warmus and, on February 14, 1991, the famous "Fatal Attraction" trial began in White Plains, Westchester County.

Douglas J. Fitzmorris was the prosecutor, David Lewis was Carolyn's defense attorney, and Judge John Carey was again presiding.

Carolyn became a media star with her femme fatale look, sparking the "Fatal Attraction" fascination. She paraded into the courthouse each day in designer clothes and sunglasses, looking like a model. She was all over the newspapers.

The prosecution's evidence included Parco's testimony (under immunity) about the gun and silencer, phone company records of the call to the gun shop, and the use of a stolen I.D. to buy a gun.

The defense was that there was a conspiracy between Paul Solomon and Vincent Parco and they faked evidence against Carolyn.

Some of the evidence included:

Warmus called Parco the day after the murder to say that some teacher had been stabbed or bludgeoned and that she had thrown her gun off the parkway

Parco admitted that he was infatuated with Warmus but he had always rejected her sexual advances

In August 1989 Warmus had asked Parco to check out a license plate number of a woman Solomon had been dating

Warmus had told Parco during the summer of 1989 that she had never had a relationship with Solomon and that she had been bowling "with a bunch of teachers" when Betty Jeanne was killed

A trucker named Anthony Gambino said that Parco had asked him in the summer of 1988 to commit a murder

A guy named Joseph Lisella said he had overheard Parco soliciting a hit

Carolyn's father claimed that Parco had tried to shake him down for a lot of money in the summer of 1989

The defense had a different version of the phone records than the prosecution did, which put in question Carolyn's call to the gun shop and backed up the defense's theory of conspiracy—the judge allowed the jury to have both versions

Paul Solomon's testimony in this trial was undermined when the prosecution elicited the fact that he had signed a movie deal for his story.

The jury deliberated for twelve days before declaring themselves unable to arrive at a unanimous verdict. They were deadlocked at eight to four in favor of conviction. Judge Carey declared a mistrial on April 27, 1991.

The jurors in favor of acquittal said they could not believe that a woman could have been so brutal as to pistol-whip the victim that way. One juror couldn't believe that a woman could hit a moving target nine times. But they all believed that the defense's phone records were forged, possibly out of desperation.

Second trial

The second trial began on January 22, 1992. James A. McCarty was the prosecutor this time, and Carolyn's new defense attorney was William I. Aronwald. Judge John Carey was again in charge of the proceedings.

The new defense approach was about reasonable doubt rather than a frame-up. They still intended to create suspicion of a Parco/Solomon conspiracy, but they knew that the jurors in the first trial had not believed most of the conspiracy evidence.

After the first trial, Carolyn was indicted for the phone records forgery, but the judge disallowed that from being brought into evidence. Why? Because it could have been her team that was responsible for the forgery, not Carolyn, and it was therefore not evidence of consciousness of guilt on her part.

The prosecution's path was the same as before. But they suddenly got a nice surprise.

A black glove that had been in the murder scene police photos, but had later disappeared, had been rediscovered. And Forensics had found finger-shaped bloodstains on the top of this glove.

Foreshadowing the O.J. trial, all manner of evidence was put forth about this glove. Where it was manufactured and who imported it. Who bought it and when. Testimony about fibers and receipts.

Kristan Solomon testified for the prosecution about what kinds of gloves Carolyn normally wore. Carolyn's stepmother Nancy Kay Dailey testified that Carolyn had lots of black gloves.

The New York Times said, "for a minute every eye shifted to the young woman at the defense table in the flowing black skirt and the black boots." Nancy said that black was not among Carolyn's favorite shades. "She looks very good in bright colors."

After the glove thing died away, the trial went back to normal. Someone testified about the silencer. There was testimony to refute the school nurse's assertion that Carolyn had talked about having a gun. The forged phone records were out, so the defense presented some theory about somebody tapping into Carolyn's phone line and making calls on her "behalf."

In summation, the defense powerfully argued that Betty Jeanne was "unwanted baggage" for Paul and also brought up the "magically" materialized glove.

The prosecution powerfully argued that there was too much evidence against Carolyn to be argued away and that Paul had nothing to gain by getting rid of his wife, whereas Carolyn had long viewed Betty Jeanne as an obstacle.

A few other pieces of evidence on the prosecution side were:

Carolyn had just found out that Kristan was away

The Solomons had attended a bar mitzvah the previous day (family thing getting in Carolyn's craw)

Carolyn's phone bill showed a call to the gun shop 30 minutes after she finished speaking to Solomon

Timing: Betty Jeanne died at 7:15; Paul showed up at Treetops on time at 7:30; Carolyn was late at 7:45 and claimed to Paul that traffic was the reason

Conviction

On May 26, 1992, after six days of deliberation, the second jury found Carolyn guilty of second-degree murder and illegal gun possession.

Jury members cited "the glove" as an important reason for their verdict.

Sentence

The minimum sentence possible for this charge was 15 years, but Judge Carey handed Warmus 25 years to life, the maximum. He said that she had committed "a hideous act, a most extreme, illegal and wanton murder."

Sexual abuse in prison and lawsuit

In 2001, a prison guard retired to avoid charges after officials accused him of having an affair with Carolyn.

This was reported by The Post in 1999: Sgt. Dominick Crisafulli, 52, was suspended for engaging in an "inappropriate relationship" with Warmus for nine months.

A stack of letters between them was confiscated, and she apparently had her parents meet him at a restaurant to give him barbecue tools as a gift.

According to The Post, the letters were passed between guard and prisoner by Warmus' private investigator and his wife, a lawyer who works for Warmus. Their visiting privileges were suspended pending the outcome of an investigation.

In April 2004, corrections officer Glenn Looney was charged with second-degree sexual abuse for having sexual contact with Carolyn in 2002. She had reportedly kept his semen refrigerated for two years to back up her accusation.

The case against Looney was about to go to trial in April 2005 when it was abruptly dismissed. Carolyn Warmus was unwilling to go forward with the case, according to a source in the Westchester County D.A.'s office.

In October 2004, Warmus filed a civil action for deprivation of rights against the Bedford Hills Correctional Facility, the New York State Department of Correctional Services, and a list of people associated with those entities. She claimed that she had been forced to have sex with guards in exchange for ordinary privileges and that she was punished with protective custody when she tried to complain.

In December 2009, the Court ordered New York State to "issue a check for $10,000 to Carolyn Warmus for deposit in her inmate account" and to pay her lawyers $69,531.53.

Status now

Carolyn is still incarcerated at the Bedford Hills Correctional Facility for Women. If she had been handed the minimum sentence of 15 years, she would have been paroled in 2007. She will be eligible to apply for parole in 2017. She will be 53.

Update on Carolyn's father

In 1990, The New York Times reported that Mr. Thomas Aloysius Warmus' net worth was more than $150 million. He owned a fleet of jets, several homes, and dozens of cars.

Sometime in the 1990s, he declared bankruptcy for himself and for American Way Service Corp.

In 2002, he was sentenced to 97 months for hiding assets from the bankruptcy proceedings.

"Warmus was found guilty of orchestrating a complex scheme to conceal assets that included high-end collectible automobiles, such as Ferraris and a Lamborghini; a 42-foot yacht; and a collectible World War II fighter aircraft. Before filing for bankruptcy, Warmus had a net worth of $50 million and his insurance companies were valued at more than $100 million. His scheme to defraud creditors began several months pre-petition when he diverted revenues from American Way Service Corp. to companies in the name of his wife and diverted his personal income to companies in the name of his business associates, wife, and mother-in-law. While in bankruptcy, Warmus continued to sell undisclosed assets and use the proceeds for his personal benefit. During the criminal trial, a trial attorney from the Miami office of the U.S. Trustee served as Special Assistant U.S. Attorney and the U.S. Trustee Program's National Bankruptcy Fraud Coordinator testified as an expert on bankruptcy matters."

In 2007, Mr. Warmus' convictions and sentences were affirmed, his appeals came to an end, and he was still incarcerated at that time.

ALYSSA BUSTAMANTE

HEIDI POOLE

Alyssa Bustamante came from a troubled family. It sparked a rage inside of her that led to one of the most shocking killings in recent memory.

Born to Michelle and Ceaser Bustamante on January 28th, 1994, her parents were cousins by marriage and her mother was only fifteen years old. They moved around the state of California before moving all the way to St. Martins, Missouri when Alyssa was two years old. Michelle wanted to be near her mother, Karen Brooke, who lived in nearby Jefferson City.

Michelle would give birth to a set of twin boys four years after Alyssa and then have another daughter. The teen mother couldn't adequately provide for her young children, however, compiling a record of petty thefts to support a drug habit. Michelle struggled to pay the rent and found herself with three misdemeanor criminal convictions for drunk driving and marijuana possession. Ceaser was even worse, routinely beating Michelle before receiving a ten-year prison sentence for an undisclosed assault charge.

"She (Alyssa) had a very troubled background," Jefferson City reporter Jeff Haldiman said. "A very troubled life. Her mother and father both had issues with drugs and drinking."

At the age of six years old, a hungry Alyssa would walk into her living room and see her mother stretched out on the couch.

Drunk and high.

"Alyssa's mother was not much to write home about," forensic psychologist Paula Orange said. "She would do drugs in from of Alyssa, one time to the point of overdosing in front of her. She would also leave the little girl to fend for herself a lot. She was the type that would say 'there's cereal and milk in the fridge.'"

The sight of her mother down and out on drugs, the absent father, and the daily neglect would prove to be too traumatic for Alyssa.

"Something in her snapped, early on her childhood," Orange said. "There are numerous stories where children are able to overcome horrendous parenting. Alyssa received a lot of help but couldn't do it."

Child protective services would eventually intervene on Alyssa's behalf. They would remove her from her mother's custody and sent to live with her grandmother.

Her grandmother, Karen Brooke, was excited to give Alyssa a second chance at life.

"The grandmother was put in charge taking care of Alyssa and her brothers and her sister by court order due to issues that Alyssa's mother had over the years," Cole County Sheriff Greg White said.

It took some time but Karen would eventually be given legal guardianship over Alyssa and her other siblings in 2002. The children would enjoy living at their grandparents' house which was on a large ranch. There was plenty of room for the children to play both on the ranch lot and in the woods nearby.

The intervention on Alyssa's behalf, however, had come too late.

LIKE MOTHER, LIKE DAUGHTER

As she got older, Alyssa would replicate the life of her mother.

She would pop pills...Tylenol, Thorazine, whatever else she could get her hands on...then lose herself in violent fantasies and suicidal thoughts.

By the age of thirteen, those suicidal ideations would come full bore as she overdosed on some psych meds mixed with some over the counter drugs.

"It was a Labor Day weekend," Haldiman said. "When she had taken an overdose and was found in the bathroom. I think that was one of the bigger warning signs for the grandmother to try and get more help for her."

"She took a bunch of Tylenol and something else," Alyssa's friend, Jennifer Meyer said. "Some sort of pain killer. This was at her grandparent's home. She passed out and her grandma found her and called an ambulance. She had to have her stomach pumped. Then she went to the hospital for awhile and they sent her to a psych ward for awhile. I know she was away from school for like two or three months."

The suicide attempt was an alarming wake-up call for Karen Brook. Alyssa was only thirteen. Teenagers trying to commit suicide certainly wasn't uncommon among teens with troubled backgrounds, but even physicians commented that they never encountered someone as young as Alyssa with her kind of thoughts.

Karen would seek help from as many third parties as she could. She would send Alyssa to several different therapists as well as a psychiatrist who started her on anti-depressants.

A DOUBLE LIFE

Despite her inner turmoil, Alyssa was a stellar student. She never took a day off from school and got nothing less than "B" grades in school. Her teachers recognized her intelligence and she did not appear to have any discipline problems.

"If you had a face to face conversation with her," White said. "You would say to yourself that this is a good choice for a babysitter. She came across very well."

Alyssa, however, had a double life.

She would play the part of the nice high school girl during the day with conservative fashion and make-up. This fooled the teachers and counselors.

But outside of school, this would change.

Alyssa could contort her face into a hard look. She had pale blue eyes which she accented with heavy black eyeliner, drawn into a Kabuki-style triangle, giving her a clownish look. She had light brown hair which sometimes ran down into her eyes. She had plenty of attitude and ran with a Goth crowd.

She fostered this alter-ego on-line, cyber-bullying people for recreation. On her social media sites, she would smear red lipstick which she made to look like vampire blood. She would snarl at the camera and grit her teeth.

SELF-MUTILATION

The angry and bizarre poses on her social media masked a bigger problem. Alyssa hated herself and wanted to cause self-harm. She would take razor blades and make incisions on her arm and wrist.

Psychologists would see this act as a form of self-medication.

Alyssa would carve pentagrams, hearts with a line going through them, and an upside down "Peace" sign. Her largest work was carving the word "HATE" across her belly in large letters.

She would do this cutting as a form of distraction. She would focus on the blade cutting into her skin, the blood coming out...and the pain. She did this as a way to take the focus off her emotional difficulties and make physical pain take center stage.

"The cutting would give her a temporary respite," Orange said. "Alyssa would find herself coming off the high of cutting herself and eventually the bad memories, bad situations, would arise once again in her mind, forcing her to cut herself again. It would become an endless cycle of self-harm."

By the time she was a teenager, Alyssa would amass over three-hundred self-inflicted cuts all over her body. She would also burn herself with matches and bite into her skin.

"There was another side to her," White said. "It was like flipping a switch, going back and forth between the two."

"It was almost like she was living two different lives," Haldiman said. "But inside something was building up. Really building up."

AN ON-LINE PRESENCE OF RED FLAGS

Alyssa would showcase her person on-line as 'badalyssa' among other pseudonyms. In one social media profile, she listed her hobbies as "cutting" and "killing people". These were more than words of bravo from an attention seeking teenager.

Alyssa meant every word.

Her YouTube account was registered under the name Okamikage which was Japanese for "Wolfshadow." She listed her location as "somewhere I don't want to be" and her profile photo showed her with the vampire-style lipstick, pointing a finger at her head like a gun.

Scars from her cutting could be seen on her wrist.

Her YouTube channel (since removed) featured several videos of both her and her brothers trying to replicate stunts they had seen in the show "Jackass". The one revealing video, however, is one that Alyssa titled "Idiots Getting Electrocuted by Electric Fence."

The video starts with Alyssa filming herself touching an electrified fence used to house cattle. She laughs and shudders at the jolt then begins coercing her younger brothers to follow her lead.

"This is where it gets good," Alyssa wrote on the YouTube video clip. "This is where my brothers get hurt."

Her Twitter messages were all dark and more than hinted at an inner rage. She wrote often of "addiction" and "terrors."

"All I want in life is a reason for all his pain," she tweeted as well as "I hate authority."

While in school, she would freak out her friends by asking bizarre questions.

"You ever wonder what it would be like to kill someone?"

But most of her friends would not take her seriously. It seemed as it seemed like idle teenage banter.

"I was at her party," Alyssa's friend Jennifer Meyer said. "And she kind of just took me off to the side randomly and she's like, 'You know, I wonder what it would be like to kill somebody,' because I guess she was mad at one of her friends there, but it just seemed kind of strange. But you wouldn't logically think one of your friends would kill somebody."

Alyssa seemed to be building herself up psychologically to kill someone, The questions and conversations with friends allowing her to psyche herself up for something she wanted to do.

"I'd like to kill her," Alyssa would say, pointing at a random person walking down the hallway at school.

Her words would eventually lead to the deed.

THE MOST INNOCENT

Just leaving a few houses down, nine-year-old Elizabeth Olten would come over to Alyssa's house to play with Alyssa's half-sister.

Elizabeth was a sweet-faced girl with a personality to match. She loved cats, the color pink and was a "girly girl." She had long brown hair and sparkling brown eyes. She was shy but friendly.

"She was somebody special," Peggy Florence said, a friend of the family. "They call her a girlie girl. She would be outside in the snow or in the mud in her frilly little dress."

"Everything that I could tell about Elizabeth," White said. "Was that she was a sweet young lady who did relatively well at school. Her classmates seemed to like her. The teachers had good reports and her mom and family loved her dearly."

"She had frequently gone to the five-year old's (Alyssa's sister) residence," White said. "So it wasn't a huge issue."

Everyone loved Elizabeth.

Everyone except Alyssa as she watched the two girl play act with dolls on the back porch, having a "tea party."

Alyssa eyeballed the young Elizabeth with one thing on her mind.

She wanted to kill her.

"I think Alyssa chose Elizabeth predominantly because it was a relatively easy target of opportunity," White said. "And that's a horrid thing."

THE KILLING TIME

In the fall of 2009, Alyssa began planning out how and when she would fulfill her sick fantasy.

She walked into the woods behind her house and began digging.

Plugging in her ear buds while listening to some death metal, she dug and dug, digging two shallow graves.

"She'd been thinking of killing for some time," White said. "And certainly had started to take significant steps toward accomplishing that end."

Alyssa dug the graves out three feet deep. Police would later speculate that she initially wanted to kill her two younger brothers and that the two shallow graves were for them. They pointed to the YouTube video in which she displayed sadistic delight in torturing her brothers by the electric fence. But when an opportunity presented itself in the form of Elizabeth Olten, she took advantage.

"Alyssa didn't care about anyone," Orange said. "Anyone or anything. She was depressed and anti-social. She hated society. She hated people."

Alyssa's diary would confirm her hatred of people and anti-social mindset. On the days leading to the murder, she would write about her cell phone battery dying. There was one long entry where Alyssa would complain about that fact that she could not call anyone to talk about the depression and rage she felt.

"If I don't talk about it," Alyssa wrote. "I bottle it up and when I explode, someone's going to die."

During this time, Karen Brooke would become increasingly worried about Alyssa. A religious woman, Karen realized that all of the counseling, therapy and medication was having no effect on Alyssa. Her granddaughter was still cutting herself and her physician raised her dose of Prozac to forty milligrams a day.

Karen would complain that the high dosage would have an altering effect on Alyssa's behavior. She would come home late when she normally would come straight home after school. She would not come down for the family evening meals, leaving her grandmother to worry about her mental state. Karen would then call Alyssa's doctor and he informed her that the higher dosage of the Prozac would take another month "to level out."

But the Prozac would have no effect on Alyssa. On October 21st, 2009, she would bring her morbid fantasies to life.

AFRAID OF THE DARK

It was starting to get dark. Elizabeth knew she had to get home or else her mother would get mad.

She said her goodbyes to her playmate then started to walk home.

Then she received a call on her cell phone.

It was Alyssa.

"Come back to the house," Alyssa said. "I have a surprise for you."

The girl trekked back to the home and Alyssa led her down the wooded path behind her home. The two walked for quite a ways before Elizabeth started to become tired and scared.

"It's getting dark," Elizabeth complained. "I want to go home."

"Don't you want your surprise?" Alyssa asked.

Elizabeth trusted Alyssa. She was older and seemed nice.

"I don't know."

"Come on, you're going to love it."

"Okay."

Alyssa put her arm around Elizabeth and led her further into the woods. The two walked and walked until the sky grew dark.

Without warning, Alyssa began to attack Elizabeth.

"Alyssa began by trying to cut Elizabeth's throat," White said. "And Elizabeth reached up and grabbed the knife, receiving defensive wounds on the inside of her fingers. Alyssa ends up dropping the knife and begins trying to strangle Elizabeth. According to her statement to us, strangling her until 'the light went out in her eyes.' And then she's down, kneeling across Elizabeth's torso and takes the knife and stabs her eight times. One time sufficiently hard to go through the breastbone, through the top part of the heart into her spine."

"This was her kill fantasy," Orange said. "That is why she tried all three methods of killing. First, she tried slicing Elizabeth's throat. Perhaps that didn't give her the feeling she craved so she began strangling the girl to death. But she needed more. She needed to know what all those fantasies felt like. So then she began stabbing the young girl. Slicing, strangling, and stabbing. She had thought about all three and wanted to know what they all felt like."

The self-harm, the self-mutilation that she practiced on herself was now transferred to harming someone else.

Someone innocent.

Her adrenaline racing, Alyssa dragged Elizabeth's body to one of the shallow graves.

"Alyssa took Elizabeth's body and rolled it to the grave and covered it up," White said. "Stringed some leaves across it and went home. Got cleaned up. Put the knife in the dishwasher."

A HAPPY KILLER

The next morning, Alyssa would write out her thoughts in her journal, expressing the euphoria at what she had done. She described how she had just killed someone, strangled them and slit their throat.

"It was ahmazing," Alyssa would write, going on to say how much she enjoyed it then ending the entry with a snarky "Kay, I gotta go to church now, lol."

Elizabeth's mother had called the police around seven p.m., about forty-five minutes after she was last seen. The community organized quickly.

The search began quickly for the girl. St. Martins, Missouri epitomized small town America. It had just over one thousand people and everyone knew each other. Volunteers began searching the woods behind the neighborhood homes.

Police pinged Elizabeth's cell phone and the GSP led them to the woods but the battery on Elizabeth's cell gave out.

The authorities knew they were close but they could not find Elizabeth.

Alyssa had done a very good job of hiding the body.

"Elizabeth was already dead before we were ever notified," White said. "It was that fast."

Everyone in town thought that an older male predator had snatched up Elizabeth.

"That was the narrative that everyone was used to," Orange said. "Everyone became frantic, talking about any strangers that they may have seen in town. But soon rumors spread that a teenager was involved. Everyone assumed it to be a teenage male."

RETRACING ELIZABETH'S STEPS

Alyssa had not shown up for school the day after Elizabeth's abduction. It was her first unexcused absence.

This raised a red flag to police as they questioned Alyssa. They brought her out back where they asked why she had dug out a grave.

Then they began searching through the house.

Alyssa acted fast. She tried to block what she had written in the diary by scratching out the words.

"We were still able to read some of the words through the writing," White said. "We put a very strong light source behind it and read her original words. At that point, she did confess to it and ultimately take us to the scene of the homicide and to the grave."

Word spread around town that Elizabeth was dead and that Alyssa was the killer.

Everyone involved went into shock. A senseless crime, a murder of an innocent.

Did this really happen?

The brutality of the crime shocked the community. An adult killing a child is rare but it has happened before. No one had ever heard of a fifteen-year-old girl killing a nine-year-old.

"When they announced they had found the body," Haldiman said. "There was an audible hush. They just couldn't believe that, nobody could believe that, number one a child was dead and number two that the person that did it was as young as she was. That just floored so many people. Everybody."

The case became even more tragic as only weeks earlier a panel of psychiatrists determined that Alyssa should be institutionalized for a long term. These clinicians knew that Alyssa was an extreme danger to both herself and other people.

Their warnings went unheeded, however, and Alyssa was returned home.

THE TRIAL

Alyssa would be put to trial and be tried as an adult.

"In this case," White said. "It was clearly, coldly planned, calculated and executed. She executed her neighbor for no reason other than she wanted to see someone die."

While awaiting trial, Alyssa went stir crazy behind bars. She began cutting herself with her own fingernails before placed on suicide watch. Her attorney motioned that she be sent to a psychiatric institution.

Her defense team worked overtime to try and explain Alyssa's murderous act. They recounted the fact that she had been on the anti-depressant Prozac and had been told to increase her dosage a few weeks before murdering the little girl. They told the jury about her upbringing of neglect, suicide attempts and the mental illnesses/drug use of both parents.

But the community-at-large wanted Alyssa's blood. Among the things they wrote were:

"What is a shame is that the Murderer did not die when she tried to commit suicide when she tried to in 2007."

"From what I've heard this girl has had mental problems for some time and has seen counselors or someone in the past."

"Either deport her or send her to the gas chamber. One less sicko wasting our tax dollars."

Prosecutor Mark Richardson would argue for Alyssa to receive life in prison plus an additional seventy-one years.

The years that Elizabeth had lost.

"These sentences are appropriate," Richardson wrote. "And fit what happened to Elizabeth at the hands of a truly evil individual who strangled and stabbed an innocent child simply for the thrill of it."

Alyssa would plead guilty to second-degree murder.

She would take the stand during her trial and betray some signs of humanity, turning to Elizabeth's mother and family.

She expressed how "horribly" she felt for what she had done. Then she suggested that if she could give her own life for Elizabeth's, she would.

The apology fell on deaf ears for both Elizabeth's family and the jury. They felt as if the apology was fake and meaningless.

"I think Alyssa should get out of jail the same day Elizabeth gets out of the grave!", screamed Elizabeth Olten's grandmother.

"She's an evil monster," Elizabeth's mother, Patty Preiss said. "So much has been lost at the hands of this evil monster. Elizabeth was given a death sentence, and we were given a life sentence. I hate her. I hate everything about her. She's not even human."

"Alyssa was pure evil," Orange said. "She told investigators that she killed Elizabeth, that darling little girl, because she wanted to see the light in her eyes go out. If that doesn't make her evil and irredeemable, I don't know what does."

"When a person plans and executes for no other reason that they want to see another person die," White said. "That person is going to re-offend. I think Alyssa is too dangerous to be out of prison.

Alyssa would be sentenced to life in prison but given the possibility of parole. She currently resides in a Missouri women's prison.

Elizabeth would receive the funeral of a beloved princess. Her casket was placed inside a horse-drawn carriage.

All of her friends and family wore her favorite color: pink.

WHEN THE GIRL NEXT DOOR KILLS: THE TRUE STORY OF TYLAR WITT

ERICA FOSTER

"At round one in the morning, the girl snuck the boy into her house. He stabbed her in her sleep, killing her and freeing themselves." This was an excerpt from fourteen year old Tylar Witt's story entitled, "The Killer and his Raven." A story she wrote about her own mother's brutal murder.

Tylar Witt lived in an upscale neighborhood in El Dorado Hills, California with her forty seven year old single mother, Joanne Witt. Joanne worked for the county as an assistant engineer for the Department of Transportation and they lived in an elegant house in a nice gated community. Tylar was a fourteen year old girl who was entering her freshman year at Oak Ridge High School. She was described as a sweet girl when she was growing up. Her mother paid for riding lessons and they liked to stay at home and watch movies and cook, but as Tylar grew up, the behavioral problems began and the fights between the mother and daughter turned into physical altercations. Tylar was turning into a different person, she was becoming a monster.

It all started out as what looked like typical teenage rebellion. Tylar embraced the emo and gothic lifestyle by wearing dark and baggy clothes, she had a love of anime and Japanese cartoons, along with everything violent and connected with death. Tylar met her 'Romeo', nineteen year old Steven Colver, at a coffee shop in the popular shopping center of Town Center Shops, where they both frequented. As Tylar was entering her first year of high school, Steven was beginning his first year of college. He was employed as a Shift Lead at Rubio's Mexican Grill. The duo quickly became inseparable. Tylar looked at the older boy as a god and worshiped everything about him. There wasn't anything she wouldn't do for him. The two were in love.

It was in April of 2009, a few weeks after the two had met, that Tylar approached her mother. She convinced her mother that Steven was gay, so that he would be allowed to rent the extra room in their family home. After much resistance from family and friends, Joanne defended the decision by saying that Steven would be helping her make the mortgage payment, as well as help Tylar with her homework. She was described as very strong-willed by her friends and family and didn't let their opinion of others affect her decision to let Steven move in. Joanne didn't suspect a relationship between Steven and her daughter until one day in May, about a month after Steven had moved in. She entered Steven's room and found Steven and Tylar about to engage in a sexual relationship, or had just finished. She found Tylar naked and hiding in Steven's closet, trying to cover herself up. Joanne was understandably upset and demanded that Steven immediately move out. She called two of her male coworkers to come over and assist her. Joanne informed them that she was kicking Steven out of her house and she didn't want to be alone when she did it in case anything were to happen. The male coworkers helped place all of Steven's belongings on the sidewalk and even threatened Steven before he left.

Vinnie Capatano, one of Joanne's coworkers helping her that day, threatened Steven, "If you make contact with Tylar again, either by phone or in person- I am going to hurt you. And I am going to hurt you East Coast style, not West Coast style." It was an act intended to promote intimidation and scare tactics. Steven looked unshaken, which annoyed Capatano even further. His words didn't seem to bother Steven at all.

Joanne was convinced that Steven had committed a crime by sleeping with her underage daughter and made that clear to Steven before he left. She threatened to go to the police and file statutory rape charges if Steven ever came into contact with her daughter again. He didn't take Joanne's words seriously, or the threats of her coworkers. Steven was later found at least twenty more times after this encounter, sneaking into Joanne's house. All Joanne wanted to do was get her daughter away from this older boy that seemed to influence her bad behavior and irrational decisions. Joanne acted as any other mother in this situation would.

Despite the threats, Steven and Tylar continued their love affair and sexual relationship during the day while Joanne was at work and late at night while Joanne was sleeping. Joanne had expressed concern to a few of her coworkers about her daughter's behavior and the boy that seemed able to control and influence her so greatly. It wasn't long until Joanne found out what was going on behind her back and continued to make good on her promise of going to the police. Steven and Tylar vowed to find a way to stay together, no matter the cost. This is the moment the plotting began between the modern day Romeo and Juliet. This was about a month before Joanne Witt was found dead in her home and arrest warrants were issued for her daughter and her daughter's boyfriend.

Joanne Witt located her daughter's diary and handed it over to the police that were handling the statutory rape complaint. The diary clearly outlined the sexual relationship between Tylar Witt and Steven Colver. It explicitly described numerous sexual positions and encounters that the two had shared. There was no mistaking that there was definitely a sexual relationship happening between Steven and Tylar. The detective called to interview Steven about the allegations and Steven claimed that he was worried about Tylar, but their relationship was platonic. He said he considered Tylar as more of a sister figure, than anything else, and he denied any sexual relationship between the two of them. He also admitted that he was scared of this whole situation and he knew she was only fourteen years old. The relationship between Tylar and her mother was volatile and destructive, to say the least, even before she turned in the diary.

Joanne was a loving and attentive single mother that made her daughter, Tylar, the center of her world. However, an incident that took place when Tylar was five years old, prompted an investigation that removed her only daughter from her home. Tylar was placed into foster care for a brief time before Joanne's parents, Norb and Judi Witt could take her in. Tylar lived with them for 6 months while Joanne attended anger management and parenting classes. The incident occurred when Tylar was just five years old after

Joanne had picked her up from daycare. The young girl was screaming in the backseat which was causing Joanne to lose patience very quickly. Joanne reached back and slapped Tylar. The daycare saw the hand shaped mark on Tylar and immediately reported the abuse to CPS, Child Protective Services.

After Tylar was finally able to go back home to her mother, Joanne was afraid to discipline her like she had before. This gave Tylar the opportunity to do whatever she wanted, knowing she could get away with it. Tylar would threaten to call CPS and report her mother again if she didn't get what she wanted. This created many behavioral problems for Tylar and this manifested itself in the violent relationship between the mother and the daughter. Tylar also reported that her mother was a heavy drinker and she would hit and punch Tylar when she was mad. These allegations were never proven. If the violence and abuse had been as severe as Tylar had made it sound, there would have been noticeable marks and bruises on Tylar. They never found any evidence of the abuse she claimed was taking place at the home. There was constant fighting and arguing. Joanne didn't feel comfortable enough start disciplining her daughter again until the few months before that led up to her murder.

The day that Joanne admitted to taking her daughter's diary into the police, was the same night that Joanne and Tylar got into a horrendous fight at home. Tylar felt betrayed by her mother's actions and began throwing objects at her and fighting with her. Tylar called 911 pretending to be Joanne in an attempt to be taken out of the home. She would have rather been in the Juvenile Detention Center than at home with her mother that night. Joanne got onto the phone with dispatch and when they asked her if she was okay, she responded no. Deputies were on their way to the residence. When the police arrived they saw a cut on Joanne's chin and several bruises. Tylar was taken in that night but was released only hours later, after Joanne refused to press charges against her daughter. Joanne was never required to go to the hospital due to her injuries.

Norbert Witt, Tylar's grandfather, claimed that Steven was a bad influence on his granddaughter, and said that he corrupted her by exposing her to sex and heavy narcotics. Steven was known to engage in illegal narcotics such as marijuana, ecstasy, and cocaine.

Norb and Judi Witt owned a luxury RV and had spent the previous two months traveling around the country. They arrived home only days before they received the call that would turn their world upside down. It was Monday when they received a call from Joanne's boss inquiring if they had any idea as to the whereabouts of their daughter. Joanne had an impeccable work history and never missed work without first calling to let them know. So, when Joanne didn't show up or call that Friday, her coworkers began to worry. They stopped by her home that night and knocked on the door, but there was no answer. Nobody seemed to be home. After Joanne didn't show up to work the following Monday either, they knew something was terribly wrong and called the police to report Joanne as missing. After speaking to Joanne's parents and informing them that they had already contacted the police, they raced over to their daughter's house, which was only a few miles away, so they could check themselves. It is there that they met the police. Norb Witt let them into the house to search. The police informed Joanne's parents that she was found upstairs in her room, and she was deceased. There was no sign of a break in or forced entry, there was nothing missing in the home. But where was Tylar? Better yet, where were Tylar and her older boyfriend?

It didn't take the police long to realize that Tylar and Steven had something to do with the cruel and heinous crime in the Witt house. It was only weeks earlier that Joanne had reported Steven to the police and turned in Tylar's diary. She made her feelings about her mother known in the words scrawled throughout the pages. Tylar even plastered her contempt for her mother across her social media sites. She wasn't shy when it came to sharing her feelings and opinion of her mother.

Tylar and Steven went on like normal the days following the murder. They were living the life they wanted now that Tylar's mother wasn't there to get in the middle of it and stop it. They were seen holding hands and kissing, and had seen some of their friends. It was after a night of smoking marijuana and doing lines of cocaine at Steven's father's house that Steven confessed to murdering Joanne and even showed his friend the bloody knife that he was hiding in the car. This friend was Matthew Wildman. Wildman later testified against Steven and told the court that Steven did indeed show him the knife that was used, and he described how the murder happened, and how Steven stood there when he was finished and watched Joanne die. Steven's father came home unexpectedly so they all left the house, with the murder weapon. The murder weapon was never retrieved after their arrest.

The couple had fled to San Francisco, they no longer cared about the consequences because their plan all along was to commit suicide. If they weren't there, they wouldn't have to face the murder charges. According to their logic, that was the only way that they would be able to stay together, without interference, as well as keep Steven out of jail because of the statutory rape charges. They thought the charges would carry a heavy prison sentence and they didn't want to risk separation due to the diary that Joanne had turned into the police earlier.

While in San Francisco, they rented a hotel room and consumed a bazaar mix of fruit loops, cake and rat poison and each had written out suicide notes. The combination of food mixed with the rat poison didn't work, however, and they were arrested shortly after, before they had a second chance to commit suicide. Alongside the food that was found in the hotel room, police also found marijuana, condoms, Steven's work apron and nametag, and the movie 'Donnie Darko' on DVD. They were found changing clothes behind a dumpster at a shopping mall in the area and were arrested by local police and taken in for questioning regarding Joanne Witt's murder.

Once in custody, Tylar refused to admit that she knew her mother was dead and admitted no fault. She asked for a lawyer and for the detectives to go away. The fateful night her mother was brutally murdered was June 11, 2009. Well into the night, after Joanne had finally fallen asleep, Tylar let Steven into the house. He had acquired a chef's knife from his restaurant job at Rubio's. Tylar had grabbed a knife out of the kitchen in her house, and the two proceeded to go upstairs to the bedroom where Joanne Witt was fast asleep. They had each planned to use the knives they had to kill Joanne....together. Tylar claimed that she could not go into the room with Steven. She fell to her knees and covered her ears, while humming to drown out the sound of her mother being stabbed to death. Steven had taken several practice slashes in the air as a warm up before going into Joanne's room and Tylar said this is what prompted her to stay outside of the room. She chose not to go in with Steven. Joanne was stabbed around twenty times. The fatal wound was a gaping slash in her neck. She struggled with her killer and had put her hands up in defense but the wounds were too severe. A bloody knife outline was left on the bed and a book entitled, "How to Parent your Out-Of-Control Teenager, was ironically nestled in the nightstand next to her bed. Tylar and Steven covered Joanne's body with a blanket, turned the air conditioner down in an attempt to preserve the body, and locked up the house and left. They decided to jump the fence instead of having to put the code in to get out. They didn't want anyone to place them there at the time of the murder.

In a suicide letter that Steven had written to his friends, as a kind of apology for what he had done, he said, "Our souls are tainted...We shall be awaiting our fate in the afterworld."

After the news of Joanne's murder got around, a neighbor spoke up about allegedly speaking to Tylar in the park a few months prior. The neighbor had been walking her daughter to the park and claimed she saw a young girl that looked alone, sad, and even angry. The girl was sitting on the swing set with her face toward the ground. She confronted her and asked what was wrong. She said the girl described a bad home life with her mother, and mentioned that her mother liked to drink and would get violent and hurt her, and they would get into a lot of fights. She said the girl seemed really cold and lost in her replies. When asked what Tylar was going to do to stop it the next time it happened she simply replied, "There isn't going to be a next time. Next time it is going to be either her or me." This statement stuck with the neighbor for a long time after. When she realized that the crime scene was a daughter that killed her mother, she finally spoke to police about the conversation in the park. The neighbor was seen on news footage talking to one of the police on the scene, but requested that her name be left out of the media.

Dan Weiner, Steven's attorney, claimed that it was not Steven that committed the murder, it was Tylar. When describing her relationship with Steven, Tylar said, "I trusted him more than I trusted anyone. And I love him more than anybody or anything. If he told me to jump off a bridge and I asked him why and he said just trust me, I would have done it." This shows just how much influence Steven had over Tylar. When neighbors of Steven's were asked to describe him they had only nice things to say.

"He's always been a nice kid as far as I am concerned. If this is true, it is out of character." –Paul Matloff. He also described Steven as a stand-up kid that never played his music too loudly and was always eager to help his neighbors.

Joan Colver, Steven's mother was quoted by reporters as saying, "He would care about others before himself. Steven is the kind of guy who would drive off a cliff or jump in front of a bullet or run into a burning building....for a friend."

When asked why Weiner felt that Steven was being targeted for performing the actual murder instead of Tylar, he didn't really know why. He backed up his defense and Steven's statement of Tylar being the one to murder Joanne Witt, given her past history compared to Steven's.

"He has never hurt anybody, or tried to hurt anybody or threatened to hurt anybody. As contrasted with Tylar who has a very specific history with her mother, and has literally threatened to kill her, to stab her...the very method by which she was ultimately killed!"

Steven had changed his story and said that Joanne was already dead by the time he arrived at the Witt house that night.

"I think realizing the gravity of the situation after being in jail for a while, it took a while before he was willing to confirm, yeah, that she had done it and how she had done it."

Steven said that Tylar stabbed her own mother to death and then called him over to the house after it was done. That is when he claims to have seen the bloody knife. He said that there was blood dripping everywhere, including some spots on Tylar's pants, but there was no evidence of blood droplets being found anywhere else in the house. It was all confined to Joanne's bedroom where she was murdered. The defense claimed that the police failed to look for blood anywhere else except for the primary focus of the house, which was the bedroom. Therefore, there was no evidence available to back up Steven's story. This new story also came about after Steven had already described to his friends how he stabbed his girlfriend's mother to death in her sleep with a butcher knife. Weiner said that Steven was not homicidal, rather suicidal. They claimed that the plan was for Steven to pick up Tylar and they would run off to San Francisco for a few days and then commit suicide together. There was no talk of murdering Joanne. The defense also mentioned that Steven had a clean record, while Tylar's was filled with a history of violence and running away. Despite the new story, Steven's confession to his friend was more than the prosecution needed. He was convicted based on his own words, just as his mother had predicted earlier.

In prosecutor Lisette Suder's words in her opening statement at trial, she described the couple's actions as "a

19 year old man and a 14 year old girl and their love affair that led to the violent almost to the point of sadistic murder of her mother." Tylar was portrayed as an extremely manipulative and brilliant girl. After lying to the detectives when she was first taken into custody and questioned, she finally decided to tell the truth and later passed a polygraph test proving it. She admitted to conspiring with Steven to kill her mother, but also said that it was Steven that committed the actual murder, while she lay in a fetal position outside of the bedroom. All of the evidence found on the scene corroborated Tylar's account of the events from that night. Tylar, in exchange for her testimony against Steven, received a reduced sentence of fifteen years to life for second degree murder. She would be eligible for parole at the age of twenty nine, instead of thirty nine. They were both sentenced at the El Dorado County Superior Court in Placerville.

Joanne Witt's brother, Michael, shared his feelings before sentencing. He was the one that had been responsible for cleaning up his sister's home after the murder. He said he would never be able to get the images of the crime scene photos out of his head.

"I hope and desire that Mr. Colver experiences the worst possible experiences our wonderful prison system can bestow upon him." The judge had tried several times to stop Matthew's rant.

The trial began with Steven still trying to protect Tylar. He didn't want people to accuse his love, Tylar, of being the mother killer. In the beginning stages of his questioning he would ask investigators if they had spoken with Tylar and he inquired about her well-being. He was sympathetic to her situation and just wanted to help her. He thought they were in it together and their love would keep them connected. It ended with the scorned lovers passing the blame to each other. Steven's defense referred to him as an easily manipulated love-struck teen.

Steven's trial lasted for four weeks but the verdict only took four hours to come back. With Tylar's account of the events, the confession Steven made to his friends, and the DNA found underneath Joanne's fingernails that linked the homicide to a male attacker, it all led Steven to a verdict of guilty, for first degree murder. He was sentenced to life in prison without the possibility of parole.

After sentencing, however, Tylar had an interview in which she admitted, "I still have a really hard time being honest. I panic when I get in trouble and the first thing I want to do is lie to get out of it." This statement could potentially be enough to seek an appeal for Steven Colver at a later date. It showed just how dishonest Tylar could be. So if she were able to say this now, what if everything she said in the trial was a lie, despite the polygraph test.

Tylar's psychologist referred to her as a sociopath. Tylar, in trial, said she had three different personalities that were living inside of her. She had her own personality, an angel named Alex, and a demon she referred to as Toby. She claimed her violent actions that led up to this point were because of the demon. Toby would come in times of intense stress. Tylar also described blackouts that she would experience when she was enraged and tried to use the compassion of her dead mother to sway the jury in her favor.

"My mom was not a vicious person and she didn't hold grudges. Even if something horrible like this would have happened, she would have asked for a just punishment. She wouldn't want to see someone suffer for the rest of their lives for a mistake they made when they were being ignorant and stupid."

The following is a letter that Tylar allegedly wrote to her mother before she was murdered. It was Tylar's plan to run away and commit suicide. It was a good bye letter addressed to Joanne.

"As much as you don't think I love you, I do. Not just because I am your daughter but because you are my best friend. Nothing I have ever said to you in anger was ever true. I would never kill you or hate you....but I can't stand to see you so unhappy, but I am growing up and seeing as you don't love me....the person I have become, I see it only fit I do one last thing to make you happy. You want me gone? I am gone."

In Tylar's testimony she admitted the act of violence toward her mother was not a spontaneous decision. It was a decision Steven and Tylar had made after thoroughly discussing their options.

"I was in shock and then I went into a full blown panic attack, hyperventilating, screaming, and shaking." This was in response to Tylar finding out that her mother had turned her diary over to the police in an attempt to build a case against Steven. They came to their own realization that the only way to save Steven from jail was to murder her mother. There was no way they wouldn't file the charges after all the proof was in the diary. They didn't see another way out.

Steven and Tylar concocted this murder plan, afraid that Steven would be sent to prison for a long time because of the statutory rape charges Joanne had filed against him. They didn't want to risk being separated from each other. They saw the murder and subsequent double suicide as a way of staying together. Just like Romeo and Juliet. What they didn't know was that the statutory rape charges only carried a year worth of prison time, if there was any time at all; it was considered a misdemeanor. Instead of a small charge, with little or no prison time, they exchanged a lifetime of freedom for a lifetime of being locked away due to their irrational nature and horrid actions that were compelled by fear. Neither Tylar, nor Steven were able to determine exactly which one of them came up with the idea of killing Joanne. Tylar had been labeled a liar from the very beginning but all of the evidence they had matched with what Tylar had been saying about that night. Everything fit into place and that's why they believed she was finally telling the truth about Steven.

During Tylar's sentencing the judge addressed her directly, "This was a brutal murder. The court has seen no emotion or even remorse for the loss of your mother...I'm sorry for you Miss Witt, because the person who loved you most and without reservation is gone."

Judi Witt had waited a long time before she would go and visit her granddaughter. When she finally set eyes on Tylar she asked how she could have done such a horrible thing. A look of shock plastered across Tylar's face and she responded, "Do you really think I would have been able to do something like this?" When asked if Judi actually believed her, she responded yes.

Not only did they lose their daughter, Judi and Norb Witt also lost their granddaughter. Judi was able to forgive a little easier than Norb. Norb has since written his granddaughter off for killing his daughter. Her actions were inexcusable. She is not the same little girl that they remembered. They said that the Tylar they knew, wasn't the Tylar that killed Joanne. They choose to remember the little girl that they first visited in the hospital after her birth. Tylar was their third grandchild. They recalled the hospital visit after her birth very fondly. They walked in there with a camera and took many pictures, in awe of their own daughter and their new granddaughter. They choose to remember Tylar as the little girl they had watched grow up, not the monster she had become after killing her own mother, not the girl that constantly defied her own mother and threatened her. Not the girl that wrote in her diary about her dream of finding out her mother had died in a car accident. Tylar had lost her way a long time ago. They choose to only remember the good, but revealed that their family was never going to be the same either. Judi and Norb had come to terms with this.

Norb finally decided to go and see Tylar, after the trial. He had refused to go and see her up until this point. When Norb entered the room, Tylar called him Poppa and embraced him. She began sobbing. Norb held onto her tightly and said, after speaking with her, he could see some kind of remorse for what she had done but he still wasn't in the position of being able to forgive her. "It is hard to forgive someone that helped kill your daughter." Norb and Judi do not visit Tylar in prison, but they do say they write to her very often.

In later interviews Tylar finally began showing small signs of remorse for her mother's brutal ending. At one time Tylar had even considered her mom to be her hero and looked at her as not only a mother figure, but also as a father figure, since she never had a real father. Tylar's personalities were all over the place. She would love her mother one day but threaten to kill her the next.

Steven's mother still holds onto the hope of her son's innocence and the possibility of an appeal. She refuses to believe that the boy she knew would be capable of doing something so unforgivable and so violent to someone else.

The tragic death of Joanne Witt and the story of her daughter and her daughter's boyfriend being the murderers shook the community. A violent history with Joanne and her defiance of any kind of authority figures led Tylar into the arms of someone she felt could protect her. The two scorned lovers had a premeditated and thought out plan to kill the object of their resistance. According to their teenage logic, getting rid of Joanne and committing suicide was the only way they could ever be together. Even the most thought out plans tend to backfire, however, and they were very much alive while Joanne was gone. They traded a life of freedom with some restrictions, for a life spent behind bars. They miscalculated the situation and now live to regret it, day after day, year after year.

WHEN GIRLS NEXT DOOR KILL : THE TRUE STORY OF MELINDA LOVELESS

IRIS OWEN

"Melinda Loveless is the closest thing you will ever look at and know what the devil is. Her eyes are empty. There's nothing inside of her." - Jacqueline Vaught, mother of Shanda Sharer.

BIRTH OF A MONSTER

Melinda Loveless was born on October 28th, 1975 in New Albany, Indiana to Marjorie and Larry Loveless. Melinda would be the youngest of three daughters born to the couple. Her father, Larry, would be a celebrated Vietnam veteran who would be given a hero's welcome in his return home. Behind closed doors, however, Larry was a certified nut who abused his wife and children.

After returning home from military service, Larry would work for the Southern Railroad before becoming a probationary officer with the New Albany Police Department. He would be fired after only eight months on the job after he and his partner would be convicted of assaulting an African-American man.

Larry would justify the assault as he believed that the man slept with his wife.

The incident would be a bit of a head-scratcher as Larry had fantasies of being a cuckold. He would bring his co-workers home to have sex with his wife so he could watch. He would also introduce his wife to a swingers lifestyle.

Larry was a hedonist. He indulged in whatever pleasurable whim his mind could dream up. This also meant spending exorbitant amounts of money. He would buy motorcycles, cars, guns, and other gadgetry. It all became too much as the couple would file for bankruptcy in 1980.

Seeking to turn his family's destiny around, Larry decided they needed religion. He would gather up Melinda and her sisters to attend the Graceland Baptist Church. Both Larry and Margie vowed to stop drinking and put an end to their swinging lifestyles. Larry would soon become a recurring speaker in the church, taking the podium and talking about how Christ had changed his life.

Bad judgment would remain at the forefront of their lives, however. They would let Melinda go with an older man to a hotel room by herself as he claimed he needed to perform an exorcism on her. Larry would become one of the resident family counselors in the church. He would talk to a troubled husband and wife privately and invariably make a pass at the women. He tried to rape one of them and was then excommunicated from the church.

After that incident, Larry decided to turn his back on religion and anything that resembled taking the high road in life. He and his wife would then resume their partying ways with booze and swinging.

CRIMINAL PERVERSIONS

Larry would state that he and his wife had an open relationship. They would enter bars together in Louisville and Larry would pretend to be in the medical field, acting like a big shot doctor or dentist. He would introduce Marjorie as his girlfriend but proceeded to hit on whichever bar girl caught his eye. He would also allow some of his friends from work to have sex with Marjorie but she found his co-workers to be repulsive.

They would have sex orgies with other couples. On one occasion, Margie tried to commit suicide afterward as the experience was so degrading.

Undaunted, Larry would direct a gang rape of Margie and she again tried to kill herself by drowning. She would deny Larry sex for over a month until one night he became so frustrated that he raped her in front of Melinda and her sisters.

Yet she remained with him.

Around 1986, the couple were again in a seedy Louisville bar with Larry chatting up two women. He wanted to take the women home but Margie would not let him. Enraged, Larry would beat his wife up so bad that she was sent to the hospital. He would later be convicted of battery.

By 1988, Larry began working for the United States Postal Service but quit after three months. He loafed around on the job and would often bring undelivered mail back to his home to burn. With little money coming in, visiting extended family would often complain that the Loveless daughters looked undernourished.

INCEST

The rumors about Larry sexually abusing his daughters remain uncorroborated. There were court testimonies that he had fondled Melinda's older sister Michelle when he was a baby. There were also allegations that he molested his wife's thirteen-year-old sister as well as Melinda's cousin for several years.

Melinda's cousin would testify in court that Larry tied all three sisters up in the garage and raped them on by one. Both of Melinda's sisters have said that he molested them but Melinda herself would not admit that it ever happened to her.

She would, however, sleep in bed with him until she was fourteen when he finally left the family.

What is certain was that Larry had a traumatizing effect on all of his daughters. On one occasion, he fired a gun in Michelle's direction when she was only seven, missing intentionally but trying to scare her. He would also take the girls' underwear from the laundry and smell it in front of family members, trying to humiliate them.

Margie would then catch Larry "spying" on a then fifteen-year-old Melinda and her friend. Enraged, she grabbed a knife and began slicing at him. He was able to wrest the knife away from her but had to go to the emergency room for injuries suffered during her attack.

"Margie had an inability to cope," forensic psychologist Paula Orange said. "She tried religion, counseling, hedonism. It all didn't work. Larry was a pervert with a personality disorder. He would run right over Margie and do whatever the hell he wanted. This traumatized Melinda obviously. Her father was abusing her and others while her mother's only response was to try and kill herself."

Margie would try and kill herself one last time but her daughters were able to intervene. Larry would then divorce Margie, wanting to start a new life. He left behind all of his daughters, remarried and moved to Florida.

Melinda took her father's absence the hardest. Larry would humor her for a little while, writing her letters.

Soon the letters stopped and their relationship deteriorated to having no contact.

"The divorce would have a great impact on Melinda," Orange said. "Her home life was horrid, obviously. She had no guidance other than her mother's Christian fundamentalism which would be offset by the way she lived her life. Melinda was raised by spiritual schizophrenics if you will. What she ultimately did was her choice but she did not have any sort of checks and balances in place when she was a child."

Melinda's father, Larry, would be arrested in February of 1993 after open court testimony revealed that he had abused his wife, daughters and their cousin. Because most of the crimes took place between the years of 1968 to 1977, all but one of Larry's charges would be dropped to the statute of limitations in Indiana. He would plead guilty to one count of sexual battery then be released in June of 1995.

He then tried suing the Floyd County Jail system for $39 million dollars. Among his primary complaints during in incarceration was that he was now allowed to sleep during the day or read the newspaper.

His lawsuit was unsuccessful.

THE DOWNWARD SPIRAL

Melinda's behavior became increasingly erratic after her father's rejection. She would get into fights at school and exhibit signs of clinical depression. At the age of fourteen, she entered into a lesbian relationship with a classmate named Amanda Heavrin. Her mother expressed anger at Melinda's sexual orientation but would eventually accept it. Melinda's relationship with Amanda, however, would eventually deteriorate.

The two were not dating when Amanda would become enamored with a younger girl named Shanda Sharer. Melinda would see the two talking outside a school dance and go into a jealous rage.

What she didn't know was that the fifteen-year-old Amanda was smitten with the twelve-year-old Shanda.

Amanda, both looked and dressed like a young boy. She cultivated a "boy band" look and had a sweet disposition that put Shanda's guard down. Shanda was a lonely wallflower at the school. She had recently transferred in and did not have any friends yet. Amanda took advantage of the situation, sending the young girl love notes, flowers and calling her one the phone.

Shanda liked boys but Amanda remained persistent. She knew that Shanda was flattered by the attention and grateful for her company. The new school was a lonely place for the young twelve-year-old.

Their friendship turned into a romance.

And Melinda Loveless could not have that. Amanda was hers and hers alone.

SHANDA SHARER

Shanda and Amanda would spend an increased amount of time together as the school session wore on. When they weren't together, they were writing each other notes or talking on the phone. Shanda's mother, however, caught wind of the relationship and did not approve. She thought Amanda was too old to hang out with Shanda, who was only twelve. The fact that Amanda was a lesbian only raised her eyebrows further.

Shanda was born in Pineville, Kentucky on June 6th, 1979 to Stephen Sharer and Jacqueline Vaught. Her parents would divorce early in her childhood and Shanda would move with her mother to Louisville when she remarried. Shanda would excel in school, receiving good grades while participating in cheerleading, volleyball, and softball. Her mother would divorce again when she was twelve and the family would move to New Albany, Indiana. She would then transfer into a Catholic school after her parents worried about her relationship with Amanda Heavrin. While at Our Lady of Perpetual Help, Shanda played on the basketball team and proceeded to get her life back in order.

"I met her in junior high," Amanda Heavrin recalled. "We became very, very close. We became really good friends."

But Amanda's feelings toward Shanda would only enrage Melinda. Shanda was the passive recipient of Amanda's attention but Melinda didn't see it that way. She would send Shanda notes, one of which read:

Amanda and I are going together and she loves me and I love her and she only wants to be friends with you. You need to accept that! You need to find you a boyfriend because Amanda is mine.

"Shanda would go up to the teacher's desk and Amanda would be staring at her," Melinda said. "I'd see her and Amanda laughing and passing notes and I'd get mad."

The jealousy would eventually come to a head at the school dance. Melinda saw Shanda talking with Amanda outside and immediately confronted her young rival.

"She tried to beat Shanda up," Amanda said. "I got between them and told Shanda to run."

Melinda would be distraught afterward. She began a letter writing campaign to Amanda.

"I want Shanda dead," Melinda wrote.

"I didn't think she was capable of murder," Amanda said. "I thought maybe she'd just try to scare her. Beat her up or something. That's the Melinda I knew. I didn't know her as being a violent person."

TEEN GIRL KILL SQUAD

Melinda wanted Shanda dead.

With murder on her mind, Melinda would enlist the aid of three of her friends. Laurie Tackett, Hope Rippey and Toni Lawrence. Three teenage girls who all had similar, troubled backgrounds. The amount of psychiatric medications prescribed to each of the four teens would be enough to supply a psych ward for a year...and together they would make for an uncontrollable, unpredictable mob.

Together, they would drive over to Shanda's house and listen as Melinda told them of her plan.

But who were these girls that were so easily persuaded to murder?

First, there was Laurie Tackett, born in Madison, Indiana in 1974. She came from a religious family as her mother was a fundamentalist Pentecostal Christian. Taking on extremist views, her mother attempted to strangle Laurie when she found out that she was changing into jeans at school. Her mother also came to Hope Rippey's house unannounced after finding out that Hope's father had given the girl's a Ouija board. She then demanded that the board be set on fire and that Hope's house should be exorcised.

Laurie's father was a convicted felon who worked in a factory. She would later claim she was molested at the ages of five and twelve. Child protective services became involved and would come to Laurie's house unannounced to ensure that she was not being abused.

Laurie would rebel against her parents and would take a profound interest in the occult. She would entertain her friends as she would pretend she was "Deanna the Vampire", acting as if she were possessed.

She would enter into a lesbian relationship at the age of seventeen and her girlfriend would introduce her to self-harm. Her mother would discover her self-mutilating scars and check her into a mental hospital. Laurie would be prescribed anti-depressants upon her release but would slice her wrists again only days later. She would then be diagnosed with borderline personality disorder after a second stint in the psychiatric ward.

Having no goals or concern about the future, Laurie would drop out of high school

An elementary school friend of Laurie, Hope was born in Madison in 1976. Her parents would divorce when she was eight and she would move with her mother and siblings to Quincy, Michigan. Her parents would get back together, however, and the family would return to Madison in 1987. She had grown up with both Laurie and Toni Lawrence and was happy to be reunited with them. Her parents were leery of Laurie, however, and wanted Hope to steer clear from her. Like Laurie, however, Hope was troubled and begin to self-harm at the age of fourteen.

Toni Lawrence rounded out Melinda's trio of killers. She was born in Madison in February of 1976. She would be molested by a relative at age nine and later raped by a teenage boy at age fourteen. The boy would not be charged with the crime, instead, the police only issued a restraining order. Toni would go into therapy after the assault but refused further treatment after a couple of sessions. She would later begin to self-harm as well as sleep around with other boys, getting a reputation as a "whore". She would try to commit suicide in eighth grade.

The stage was set as Melinda had assembled a group of young girls that were just as damaged as she was. Girls that were ticking time bombs. Alone they would have done nothing violent. But together? Together they would be capable of the most horrific crime imaginable.

"Everything that horrible that happened to each of those girls," Shanda Sharer's mother, Jacqueline Vaught said. "Everything that happened to them, they took it out on my child. I think that's what they were doing, I think they just all exploded that night."

The four teenagers drove around the Indiana back roads as Melinda detailed her plan. Laurie was in the driver seat as she was the only one old enough to drive. All piled in, Melinda would tell her acolytes of her plan to scare a girl named Shanda. She pulled out a kitchen knife from her jacket and showed it to the girls.

She's a copycat," Melinda said. "I want to scare her for stealing my girlfriend."

"I'm tired of hearing you just talk about hurting her," Laurie said. "If you really want to hurt her you should go ahead and really do it."

Melinda took the challenge. She needed a volunteer to lure Shanda out of the home. She knew that Shanda's parents were no longer allowing her to see Amanda anymore. But if they could use Amanda as bait, they could lure her out.

Melinda knew Shanda's address but the girls got lost a few times and stopped to ask for directions.

Finally arriving at the home, Melinda sent Hope Rippey to the door.

Jacqueline Vaught came to the door and saw Hope in front of her. She had never seen the teen before but didn't think anything wrong when Hope politely asked if Shanda was home.

"Shanda had never been anywhere where we didn't know where she was or who she was with," Vaught said. "Shanda was not allowed to go to anybody's house where I didn't call the parents that I didn't go there. I was very, very protective."

She called Shanda down and left the teen girls alone.

"Your friend Amanda is upset and really needs to talk with you," Hope said.

"Why?" Shanda whispered, looking back to make sure her mother wasn't listening. She was no longer allowed to have anything to do with Amanda.

"She's waiting for you at the Witches Castle."

Shanda knew that Hope was referring to an old, stone house, located on an isolated hill next to the Ohio River. It was a creepy but teens like to hang out there.

"I'm having nothing more to do with Amanda."

"Have a heart," Hope said. "You must care about her, couldn't you be there for her just one last time?"

"Why did Amanda send you instead of coming herself?"

"Amanda knew she couldn't come to your house."

"I can't go now," Shanda said, looking behind herself again. "My parents are up. I'll sneak out around midnight if you want to come back hen."

Hope agreed and returned the car without Shanda.

Melinda immediately confronted Hope on why she didn't have Shanda with her. Hope explained that Shanda agreed that if they came back at midnight, she'd be willing to come with them.

The teens then head out to a nearby punk rock concert. Both Toni and Hope get bored and have sex with two boys they've just met to pass the time.

Midnight rolled back around and the girls returned to Shanda's home.

"I can't wait to kill Shanda," Melinda said. "I'd like to fuck her."

Melinda then hid in the back seat. The other girls covered with a jacket and trash from inside the car.

Hope then went and got Shanda.

"They were not mean looking, dirty child molesters," Shanda's mother, Jacqueline Vaught said. They were two children that looked like her. They said just walk twenty-five feet and talk to her. And that's what she did."

Shanda squeezed into the front seat, sitting in between Laurie and Toni. The girls pretended to like Shanda at first but soon she began feeling uncomfortable.

"The Witches Castle is a short drive away," Laurie said. "You know the legend? That house had once been owned by nine witches who had controlled the town and the townspeople had burnt the house to get rid of the witches."

"So what's up with you and Amanda?" Hope asked, turning to Shanda.

"We'd been going out for quite awhile," Shanda said. "I really cared about her."

"I see."

"What's wrong with Amanda?" Shanda asked. "Why does she have to see me so badly?"

"Surprise!" Melinda screamed, jumping out from the backseat. She grabbed Shanda's hair, pulled her head back and put the knife to the young girl's throat.

"Please don't hurt me," Shanda said.

The girls all laughed.

Laurie stepped on the gas...

CRUEL AND SADISTIC

"Bitch," Melinda hissed as she pressed the knife down on Shanda's throat. "Don't move, don't make a sound."

They arrived at the Witches Castle, parked and pulled Shanda inside. Melinda tied up Shanda's hands with a rope. Hope waved the knife in front of Shanda's face, taunting her. Laurie took along an old t-shirt and set it on fire.

"You see that?" Laurie held up the burning shirt before the crying Shanda. "That's what you're going to look like before the night is over!"

Melinda then ripped off Shanda's necklace and bracelets. She handed them to Toni and they took turns admiring the items. Hope ripped off the Mickey Mouse Musical watch from Shanda's wrist and put it in her pocket.

Several cars passed before the castle and then the girls went quiet, waiting for the coast to clear. Not satisfied that they would have total privacy, the girls dragged Shanda back to the car and stuffed her in the back seat, covering her with a blanket.

Laurie made a pit stop at a gas station while Melinda stood guard over Shanda. Hope went inside to pay for the gas while Toni makes a phone call.

She does not tell the person she is calling about the kidnapping or ask for help.

The girls then go back to their hometown of Madison, Indiana, an hour away.

Once there, they drove a few miles past Laurie's home and pull off into a seldom used logging road. Laurie stops the car and they all get out. Hope and Toni complain about the cold and wait inside the vehicle.

Melinda then hauled out Shanda from the back seat. The girl resisted until Laurie came to help and they muscle her out of the vehicle, throwing her to the ground.

"Take your clothes off, bitch," Melinda screamed.

Crying, Shanda complied with the request. Hope and Toni watch from the car window.

Melinda then took Shanda's clothes and threw them into the back seat. "I want them as souvenirs.

Playing along, Hope put on Shanda's polka dot bra. Toni turned on the radio.

"Shanda had hugged me," Laurie said in a December 1992 interview. "She asked me not to let Melinda do it. She was crying. There wasn't anything I could do."

Laura instead held Shanda's hands behind her back. Melinda then began punching the little girl.

"Please let me go," Shanda screamed. "I'll stay away from Amanda."

"Shut up!" Melinda punched Shanda hard in the stomach. She followed this up by pulling her by the hair as she fell to the ground. Shanda was prone and Michelle repeatedly kneed her in the mouth

Shanda winced and yelped in pain.

Her adrenaline and nerve increasing, Melinda took out her knife and tried to cut Shanda's throat. The blade is too dull, however.

"Get over here, Hope!" Melinda commanded.

Hope obeyed and Melinda ordered her to help hold Shanda down. Melinda then tried to use her foot to pierce the knife through Shanda's throat.

The girls then took turns stabbing Shanda in the chest.

The knife was still too dull.

"We need to just strangle her," Laura said, taking the rope and wrapping around her neck.

"Please don't kill me," Shanda pleaded.

Melinda just laughed. She sat on her Shanda's legs as Laura straddled her chest, tightening the rope.

Shanda would pass out and the girls thought she died. They picked up her body and tossed her in the trunk of the car.

POINT OF NO RETURN

The girls would arrive at Laura's home, triumphant. They would go upstairs to Laura's bedroom and drink soda. Laura, the occult aficionado, would take out her "runes stones" and perform a "future reading" for the girls.

"Our futures look good," Laurie said until they heard her dog barking outside. The teens rushed to the window and listened. They could hear Shanda screaming from the trunk of the car.

Laura went to the kitchen and got a paring knife. She hurried outside, opened the trunk and began stabbing Shanda repeatedly. The girl quieted down and Laurie closed the trunk again.

Laurie returned to her bedroom, covered in blood. She washed herself up and then addressed the kill squad with a renewed need for cruelty.

"We have to go for a ride," Laurie said.

"I'm tired," Toni said.

"Me too," Hope agreed.

Melinda and Laurie dismissed the girls and went for a drive by themselves. They headed back to the isolated road, parked and then went to check of Shanda had died yet.

The little girl sat up. Her eyes rolled in the back of her head. She tried to speak but was only to say one word.

"Mommy."

AN ENDLESS NIGHT OF TORTURE

Laurie picked up a tire iron from the trunk and bashed Shanda across the head. She closed the trunk again and they drove along the back roads. The mood turned somber and silent until they once again head Shanda choking in the back trunk.

Laura stopped and got again, opening the trunk and bashing Shanda in the head the tire iron once more. This time, a chunk of flesh from Shanda's temple went flying into the night air.

Laurie came back to the car, blood splattered across her arms.

"She looked as though she was painted red," Laurie laughed, waving the bloody tire iron and under Melinda's nose who smelled it with glee.

Melinda and Laurie then go back to Laurie's home. The woke up Toni and Hope, laughing and filling them in on how much further they tortured Shanda. The foursome discussed what they should do with the body until Laurie's mother woke up.

She berated her daughter for being out so late then yelled at her even more for having her friends spend the night without asking.

After her mother's lecture ended, Laurie led the girls to the back of her house.

ONE LAST ACT OF EVIL

"There's a burn pile out here ," Laura said, skipping through the woods beyond her back yard. They would find the burn pile but it would be covered in frost.

"That won't work," Laura said. "We're going to need some gasoline."

The girls went back to the car and opened the trunk, needing another look at their victim.

Toni refused to look at the tortured body of Shanda, shocked by the amount of blood covering the girl.

"Start the car and rev the engine if she starts screaming," Laurie said.

Hope grabbed a bottle of Windex in the trunk and began spraying Shanda's body.

"You're not looking so hot are you?" Hope taunted.

Shanda was semi-conscious. She sat up, her naked body covered in dried blood.

"Laurie!" Laurie's mother called out.

"Shit," Laurie slammed the trunk lid on Shanda's head and went to find out what her mother wanted.

After a few minutes, Laurie returned and the girls drove to a gas station. Laurie ordered Toni to buy a two liter Pepsi bottle from inside. She came back and Laurie emptied the bottle into the dirt then filled it with gasoline.

"We could get rid of her out by Lemon Road," Hope offered.

Laurie followed Hope's directions, driving onto the old country logging road. Toni would remain in the car as the three other girls pulled Shanda out from the vehicle.

Hope would pour the Pepsi bottle filled with gas over Shanda. Laura lit a match and tossed it on the body.

The fire blew high. The girls giggled and ran back to the car, speeding away.

"Wait," Melinda said. "Turn the car back around."

"The way it was told to me," retired detective Steve Henry said. "Was that they drove away and turned around and came back past the body thinking that she would be burned completely up and there would be no trace of her and she was still there so Melinda set her on fire again."

Laurie complied, doubling back and stopping in front of the burning body. They watched for a few minutes until Melinda stepped out of the vehicle with the Pepsi bottle.

She looked down on Shanda, her body in a fetal position. Tongue lolling in and out of her mouth as she convulsed in pain.

Melinda poured the remainder of the gas on Shanda and tossed another match on the little girl.

The teens then drove off and ate breakfast at a McDonald's.

"What does this remind you of?" Laurie asked as she held up a piece of sausage.

"Shanda's body," Melinda laughed. "Burned to a crisp."

Shanda was not dead yet, however. Soot was later found in her airways which meant that she was burning in the fumes around her. She was conscious while they set her on fire.

"They didn't know how to tell me how she died," Shonda's mother, Jacqueline Vaught said. "And I saw it on television. That she'd been burned alive. I didn't know that."

Melinda would then call her ex-girlfriend, Amanda Heavrin and confess to the crime.

"She told me everything that happened," Amanda recalled. "I thought it was a joke. Because I just cannot fathom that four little girls would do this to another human being. This is stuff you wouldn't even do to an animal."

She thought that if she removed the competition that she could have Amanda.

CONFESSION AND TRIAL

Toni Lawrence would be the girl to come forward and confess. She came home hysterical, telling her parents what happened. They took her down to the police station and she told detectives what happened.

All four teenagers would be charged as adults. This forced them to accept plea bargains as they wanted to avoid the death penalty.

The defense played on the fact that all four girls were victims of physical and/or sexual abuse in their childhood. Hope, Toni, and Laurie had histories of self-harming behavior. Laurie was clinically diagnosed with a borderline personality disorder and had both visual and auditory hallucinations.

Toni would cooperate in exchange for a lesser sentence. She was allowed to plead guilty to one count of criminal confinement which got her a maximum sentence of twenty years. Hope would be sentenced to sixty years with ten years suspended for mitigating circumstances plus ten years of medium-supervision probation. She would continue to appeal and the judge would reduce the sentence to thirty-five years. Both Laurie and Melinda wold be sentenced to sixty years and sent to the Indiana Women's Prison in Indianapolis.

Melinda's attorney would appeal for her release in October of 2007. He would argue that Melinda had been "profoundly retarded" by the abuse she suffered during childhood. He further argued hat she had not been competently represented during her initial sentencing. He also played the "age card", as Melinda was only sixteen years old when she entered the plea agreement with the state of Indiana and needed consent from a parent or guardian.

The appeal for her release was denied but the sentencing was reduced down to make her eligible for parole in fifteen years. It is becoming apparent that Melinda and Laurie could be released from prison as early as 2022.

Toni would be released from jail in December of 2000 after serving nine years. She would remain on parole until 2002. Hope was released from the Indiana Women's Prison on April 28, 2006, serving for fourteen years.

"None of these girls were born murderers," Vaught said. "They weren't born to murder children. They weren't born to be in prison. This what we do as parents. We mold our children into what they are."

Shanda's father, Stephen, would die at the age of 53 due to alcoholism. Stephen had become depressed over the death of his daughter and subsequently "drank himself to death" over the years.

"Steve could not have been a prouder father," Vaught said. "Shanda was his life. From the day that she died he did everything he could to kill himself beside put a gun to his head. And finally he drank himself to death and he died at fifty-three."

"Melinda has cheated me out of being with my daughter during this life. It is my wish for you (Melinda) that you live your life with memories of her screams and sign of her burned and mutilated body. I hope and pray you remember these words for the rest of your life: May you rot in hell."

www.ingramcontent.com/pod-product-compliance
Lightning Source LLC
Chambersburg PA
CBHW030241160726
47987CB00020B/488